Sam's Civil War
Marching with Sherman

by

Peter Andrew Nielsen

Bloomington, IN  Milton Keynes, UK
authorHOUSE®

AuthorHouse™
1663 Liberty Drive,
Suite 200
Bloomington, IN 47403
www.authorhouse.com
Phone: 1-800-839-8640

AuthorHouse™ UK Ltd.
500 Avebury Boulevard
Central Milton Keynes, MK9 2BE
www.authorhouse.co.uk
Phone: 08001974150

© 2007 Peter Andrew Nielsen. All rights reserved.

No part of this book may be reproduced, stored in a retrieval system, or transmitted by any means without the written permission of the author.

First published by AuthorHouse 6/11/2007

ISBN: 978-1-4343-0315-8 (sc)

Library of Congress Control Number: 2007902428

Printed in the United States of America
Bloomington, Indiana

This book is printed on acid-free paper.

Foreword

The purpose of this book is to follow the military career of Samuel B. Heizer as closely as possible. The focus, then, is fairly narrow and does not attempt to give a through presentation of the events in which he was involved. Because of his placement in the Fifteenth Corps of the Army of the Tennessee he was in the middle of the western campaign. Two major sources were used in retracing Sam's military career. The letters written by Samuel B. Heizer and the *Memoirs of General William T. Sherman* were used. Starting at Vicksburg in December of 1862 until the end of the war Sam, in some form or other, was under the leadership of General Sherman. Several Internet sources were very helpful. These sources cover the regimental history of the 30th Iowa, the XV Corps of the Army of the Tennessee, and a brigade commander's official report of the Battle Above the Clouds, and Missionary Ridge.

INTRODUCTION

Samuel Brown Heizer was born in Ross County Ohio and raised in Kossuth, Iowa. He was the son of Nathaniel Heizer and Elizabeth Brown Heizer. Sam was born February 22, 1842 and passed away on August 6, 1924 at Mediapolis, Iowa. Sam married Martha Canfield October 3, 1865. They built a house in Mediapolis, Iowa which is a few miles west of Kossuth and raised six children. Sam's youngest daughter, Grace, lived with her mother and father until they passed away and continued to live in the family home until her death in 1966. Sam's Civil War Letters were found in the Heizer family home by Sam's granddaughter and were passed on to Sam's great-grandson both of whom live in the State of Washington.

Sam volunteered for the Union Army in the summer of 1862 when he was 20 years old. He was trained at Keokuck, Iowa in the southeast corner of Iowa located on the Mississippi River. He served under General Sherman at Vicksburg during which he was at Milliken's Bend, Jackson and the Black River Bridge. Sam fought at Missionary Ridge near Chattanooga, Tennessee. He was at the Siege of Atlanta, Georgia and marched with Sherman to the sea at Savannah. Sam continued with Sherman north through the Carolinas and finishes his letters on May 21, 1865 at Alexandria, Virginia overlooking the capital in Washington D.C.. After a review of the troops May 24, 1865 by General Sherman, Sam was mustered out of the army and returned home to Mediapolis, Iowa.

In Iowa Sam worked as a teacher, a county assessor, and insurance representative with The Home Insurance Company of New York and was a Notary Public.

Sam had two brothers who were also in the Civil War. Martin Luther Heizer was in the same company as Sam and is referred to often in Sam's letters. David B. Heizer was in the 14th Army Corps. One of David's letters home was sent to Sam who copied the letter when it was sent to him. This letter was saved and is included with Sam's letters.

Contents

Foreword v
Introduction vii

Chapter One
The Beginning and Vicksburg 1

Chapter Two
The Battle for Chattanooga 11

Chapter Three
The March to Atlanta 25

Chapter Four
The Battle for Atlanta 31

Chapter Five
The March to The Sea 43

Chapter Six
The March Through the Carolinas 53

Chapter Seven
The Grand Review 63

Part Two
The Civil War Letters of Samuel B. Heizer 71

Part Three
Visual and Supplementary Material 137

Maps 139
Photographs 149
Documents 153
Letter Analysis 161
Sam's Commanders 171
The History of the 30th Iowa Regiment 175
General William T. Sherman 179
Army of the Tennessee 181
Union Army 15th Corps 183
Army Organization 187

Western Theater Engagements (Limited) 189
War Theater Comparisons (Limited)................................193
Bibliography 195

CHAPTER ONE

THE BEGINNING AND VICKSBURG

The Thirtieth Iowa Infantry regiment was organized at Keokuk, Iowa and mustered September 20, 1862. They were then moved to St. Louis, Missouri on October 25, 1862. From there, they were moved to Helena, Arkansas and were attached to the District of Eastern Arkansas, Department of Missouri until December 1862. The Thirtieth Iowa was in the Second Brigade, First Division, District of Eastern Arkansas, Department of Tennessee in December 1862. They were then regrouped to the Third Brigade, Eleventh Division, Right Wing in the Thirteenth Army Corps Department of Tennessee in December 1862. The army shortly after this was again reorganized. The Thirtieth Iowa then became part of William T. Sherman's Fifteenth Army Corps. The Thirtieth was in the Third Brigade, Fourth Division in January 1863 during Sherman's Yazoo Expedition.[1] An old newspaper clipping reported that in the first three months of the war, Sam was in the First Iowa.

Sam's unit was involved in an expedition from Helena, Arkansas to Arkansas Post from November 16 to 21. Then they were with General A. P. Hovey in an expedition to Granada, Mississippi from November 27 to December 5.

In 1862, in the Western Theatre of the war, the Union forces were pushing north up the Mississippi River from the Gulf of Mexico. They were also moving southward from Illinois along the river. In December 1862, the focal point of operations was centered on Vicksburg, Mississippi.

Vicksburg was located on a severe bend of the Mississippi on a high bluff of about 300 feet. North of the city, the Yazoo River flows into the Mississippi. The area is marshy, making military operations difficult. The Big Black River flows basically north to south a few miles east of Vicksburg, and empties into the Mississippi River at Grand Gulf, thirty to forty miles south of Vicksburg. At this time, Vicksburg was the key city controlling river traffic on the Mississippi River. Capturing the city would divide the Confederacy, preventing supplies from moving from the west to the east.

Confederate Lieutenant General John C. Pemberton was in charge of defending Vicksburg. General Joseph E. Johnston was the superior commanding officer in the West.

General Ulysses S. Grant was in command of the Union Army of the Mississippi in the West. Major General William T. Sherman was in charge of the XV Corps Department of the Tennessee.

One of the earlier actions against Vicksburg was the Yazoo Expedition. The Union army wanted to attack the city from the north along the Yazoo River waterway. General Sherman took a force of 30,000 men down the Mississippi River to the mouth of the Yazoo River, north of Vicksburg. The army was moved by boat under the direction of Admiral David Porter. The plan was to attack Chickasaw Bluffs, located northeast of Vicksburg. General Sherman was counting on the element of surprise to carry the battle.

On December 26, Sherman's forces landed on the south bank of the Yazoo River, four miles northeast of the Chickasaw Bluffs. Swampy ground made progress slow. They arrived at the bluffs on December 28. Upon deployment, General Steele, Sam's general, found himself out of position and was ordered to the west side of Chickasaw Bayou. In his countermarch, General Steele had to use steamboats to cross the Yazoo to firmer ground. On December 29, the troops were ready. The enemy's forces were estimated at 15,000. General George W. Morgan was to pass the bayou with General Fredrick Steele in support. About noon, the order was given to begin the attack. General Sherman's forces were met with heavy return fire. Sam's Third Brigade under Brigadier General John M. Thayer, Fourth Division, took a wrong turn and did not cross the bayou. This attack failed. On December 30, General Steele's forces were to proceed upriver by steamboats to Haines's Bluff and attack the hills at daylight. A thick fog, however, covered the river and made movement impossible. General Sherman decided to withdraw and by January second his forces were aboard the steamboats to return to Milliken's Bend on the Mississippi.[2]

Shortly thereafter, Major General J. A. McClernand arrived and assumed command over Sherman. This took place January 4, 1863. Since the field command would fall to McClernand if Grant directed the Vicksburg campaign from Memphis as he had intended, Grant decided to assume command himself. On January 30, 1863, Grant took direct command of the army.

In January 1863, the western armies were organized into five groups. General Sherman was in command of the Fifteenth Corps Department of the Tennessee. Samuel Heizer was in the Third Brigade Fourth Division, but was shifted to the Third Brigade First Division in February 1863. Sam wrote a letter written on March 2 from opposite Vicksburg. General Frederick Steele was then the commander of the First Division Fifteenth Army Corps.

On January 18, generals McClernand and Sherman were ordered to return to Vicksburg to work on a canal on a peninsula of land opposite Vicksburg.[3] Sherman had two divisions at work on the canal, furnishing alternately groups of 500 men a day to labor on the canal. The canal was to bridge a bend in the Mississippi River to allow ships to pass without having to follow the river past Vicksburg's gun batteries. The work was difficult and discouraging. Sherman felt the canal was a waste of human labor, but President Lincoln wanted it, so the project continued. Eventually the project was deemed unworkable and abandoned.

Sam's division had worked on the canal. In his letter of March 2, 1863, he wrote about several incidents in regard to operations during that time. One of the events was the celebrated floating of a fake gunboat down the Mississippi River past Vicksburg. For some background, the situation developed like this: In the first part of February, Admiral Porter made an attack on Confederate shipping on the Red River. The ram *Queen of the West* did considerable damage to the Confederates but ran aground and was captured. The *Indianola* was sent down the Mississippi by Admiral Porter, and in a violent battle, was beached and surrendered. Admiral Porter then took an old coal barge and made it look like a gunboat. The Confederates were completely fooled, causing four Confederate vessels to scurry downriver to safety. In his letter of March 2, 1863, Sam described what was going on:

> A report came to camp yesterday that a boat bearing a flag of truce had landed near us from the rebels and some of the boys thought they saw a white flag floating on the courthouse over the river, but my eyes could not see it. I think they were badly fooled and told them so. It almost made some of them angry when they felt sure they saw it with their own eyes. There is no doubt that two of our best boats are captured, the Steamer Ram *Queen of the West* and the gunboat *Indianola*. So much for the strategical movement of running the blockade. The rebels I have no doubt expected such a movement and prepared for it. From a parole prisoner belonging to the 26th Iowa from up the Arkansas River we have

The Beginning and Vicksburg

the report that Arkansas Post is again strongly fortified. If this be true we may have another brush there. Proctor was down to the mouth of the canal below town and he says our men are building a strong fort there. How many guns it was to contain I do not remember; but its strength must be great. The canal is being enlarged as I suppose the newspapers have already informed you and now I have some confidence in the concern. Oh and must tell you a little circumstance that occurred last week. Our regiment was then all on picket duty below the canal. One evening we saw something coming down the river near our position. It looked very much like a gunboat and some thought it really was a gunboat. We soon found that it was only a wooden concern made just like a gunboat to deceive the rebels. The Rams which the rebels captured from us which were lying a few miles below skedaddled as soon as they saw this thing coming. We found on close observation that the boat was constructed entirely of wood and logs placed in the portals for guns. It did us great service in as much as there were no cannon with us and while the Rams were down the river a battery of guns were planted to defend the place and protect the men that were working on the canal. Had this not been done the rebels might have shelled us out and done mischief on the canal. They were so badly deceived that they continued to fire at her until she was out of range of their guns.

The bayou "experiments" had failed. The possible plans to travel from the north through Grenada to Jackson, Mississippi to attack Vicksburg from the east or to take the higher ground between the Yazoo River and the Big Black River were scrapped. Diverting the flow of the Mississippi River with the canal was found to be unworkable. Grant then decided to move the army down the west side of the Mississippi River about twenty miles and ferry his troops over near Bruinsburg and Grand Gulf. As Grant moved troops southward, Sherman and his XV Corps remained at Milliken's Bend on watch for any lapses in the defenses of Confederate General Pemberton in Vicksburg.

On April 16, Admiral Porter sent a convoy of twelve vessels downstream past the Vicksburg batteries. This was done after dark and as quietly as possible. The vessels were soon discovered, and fires lit up the night sky, exposing the convoy. The convoy took two and a half hours to pass the batteries, losing one transport and a couple of batteries. The vessels that got through would be available to ferry Grant's army across the river.

General Grant had craftily planned a number of diversions to mask his planned crossing of the Mississippi at Grand Gulf. The chief of these actions was Grierson's Raid, a cavalry action through the heart of Mississippi from north to south. Sherman was to make a demonstration against Haynes Bluff north of Vicksburg to help cover Grant's movements. Sherman took ten regiments from General Blair's division to make the demonstration. Samuel Heizer was in Frederick Steele's first division, and so was not involved in this action. Afterward, Blair's division stayed at Milliken's Bend to protect the depots there, while Sherman marched with Steele's and Tuttle's divisions, following General McPherson's Corps after they had passed Richmond.[4]

General Sherman's route was to Richmond and Roundabout Bayou, reaching the Mississippi at Perkins's plantation. It was from Perkins's plantation that Sam wrote his letter of May 24. On the sixth of May, they went by a plantation called Hard Times, about five miles from Grand Gulf. With the help of the *Forest Queen* and several gunboats, Sherman got his troops across the river during May 7 and marched eighteen miles to Hankinson's Ferry. Sherman's troops were the last command to cross the river. Sherman overtook Grant at Auburn. From there, they marched north to get between Confederate General Pemberton at Vicksburg and General Joe

The Beginning and Vicksburg

Johnston at Jackson. Grant had ordered Sherman to take the right-hand road where the road split off. This road took him through Mississippi Springs and Clinton, en route to Jackson. On the way to Jackson, Major General James McPherson's XVII Corps encountered a small Confederate force under Brigadier General John Gregg near Raymond. After spirited resistance, the Confederates fell back to Jackson. The Confederates under General Joe Johnston retreated through Jackson on the Canton Road leading northward.

General Sherman stayed in Jackson one day (May 15) to tear up railroad tracks, and to destroy the arsenal, a foundry, and a cotton factory. On May 16, 1863, Sherman received orders from General Grant to proceed to Edward's Depot, where a battle was expected. The first division sent was General Steele's division, which was Sam's division. The Battle of Champion Hills was fought that day (the sixteenth) with the Federal forces of General McClernand and General McPherson fighting Confederate General Pemberton. Sherman's Corps was intercepted en route by a staff officer from General Grant near Bolton. He was told to push on to Vicksburg, crossing the Big Black River near Bridgeport. The river was crossed by pontoon bridge, and Sherman marched toward the defenses of Vicksburg. He then had control of the peninsula between the Big Black and the Yazoo rivers.

The Confederate battery at Haynes Bluff was found abandoned, and then controlled by the Federals. After a rest of a couple of hours, Sherman continued his march toward Vicksburg. On May 18, 1863, General Blair of Sherman's corps closed up against Vicksburg's defenses. As General Steele's division arrived, they were ordered to descend a bluff and make contact with the fleet on the Mississippi River. Upon reaching a road at the foot of the hills which led from Haynes Bluff to Vicksburg, Steele's forces intercepted wagons and prisoners coming from Haynes Bluff.

Sherman's XV Corps had the right side of the line of investment as they faced Vicksburg. On the nineteenth of

May, Grant ordered an assault on Vicksburg. The Confederate defenses were strong and well-manned, and Sherman's losses were heavy. A second assault was ordered for the twenty-second of May. Steele's division was to make a strong demonstration about a mile to the right of Sherman's forces toward the river. The assault was to begin at 10:00 AM. As the Union forces charged, the Confederates rose up from their parapets and delivered a withering fire upon the advancing troops. The bloody battle lasted about two hours, and at every point the Federals were repulsed. The results were about the same for the other commanders, generals McPherson and McClernand. After the battle, the Union forces took the position of a siege, which was completed by May 31.

In his letter to his parents written on May 24, 1863, Samuel Heizer described the battle of the twenty-second:

> You will no doubt hear of the dreadful but unsuccessful charges on our enemies works in this place day before yesterday, in which our regiment was engaged and in which we lost our Colonel and Major and 10 others and had 60 men wounded several of whom will doubtless die and one missing, before you read this. Our company suffered more than any other in the regiment. Losing out of 26 that went into the charge three killed and 13 wounded. Although since we came here our loss has been three killed and 14 wounded. Besides these our Captain and five men were knocked down by the explosion of shells but are now running about and not reported wounded. Our dead are Sergeant S. S. Perry and John E. Shapp and Patrick Ward. The wounded are R. P. Wycoff, Cyrus Hedges, T. U. Husted, W. H. Barnhill, T. F. Davis, J. T. Earnest, D. W. Hixon, R. B. Hixon, Wm. U. Vaugh, Joseph Loyd, J. G. Bayles, G. H. Hully, and Wm. Stewart. All these were wounded and three killed in a few minutes. T. Speed Smith was slightly wounded Monday evening.

The Beginning and Vicksburg

We have now present all told sick and well 31 men. Last night our regiment together with the rest of our brigade were moved back from the enemy's works some distance. When we stacked arms when we halted we had but ten well men to stacked arms. It seemed as if Company C was all gone. The place of the charge could not have been much worse for a charge if the rebels had made it being a high bluff and very steep with a short slope near the top not so steep. On this slope the men were butchered. General Thayer cried like a child when he saw the slaughter. I understand he was opposed to the charge in the first place. Some other regiments suffered about as bad as ours. Captain Roberts now commands the regiment Lieutenant Colonel Torrence being at Milliken's Bend. But I have not much time to write. I escaped without a scratch...

General Pemberton had about 30,000 men inside Vicksburg. General Joe Johnston was gathering a strong force near the Big Black River to threaten the rear of the Union Army. General Grant assigned Sherman to counter General Johnston, in case he should try to cross the Big Black River and threaten the Union troops in siege. General Sherman took a position west of the Big Black River, which discouraged Johnston from making an attempt to break the siege. Sherman was there from June 20 to July 4.

The Union forces continued to shell Vicksburg. A tunnel was built, then loaded with explosives. When detonated, the explosion created a large crater, through which the Union forces tried to advance. After three days of fighting, the Federals retired. Three days later, on July 1, another explosion was tried in the same area, but the results were not satisfactory and the idea was abandoned. On July 4, General Pemberton surrendered to General Grant, which put Vicksburg under Federal control.

After the surrender of Vicksburg, Joe Johnston pulled his troops back in retreat and was pursued by Sherman, who crossed the Big Black on July 5 and 6. By the tenth, Johnston had been driven into Jackson. On the eleventh, the Federals began shelling the town. Sherman's troops held the center of the line. The morning of July 17, Jackson was found to be evacuated. General Steele's division (Sam's) was sent as far as Bolton in pursuit, a distance of fourteen miles. The troops then returned to Vicksburg, and General Grant directed Sherman's corps to encamp near the Big Black River for the rest of the summer. His troops were encamped by July 27.

After the Vicksburg campaign, President Lincoln promoted General Grant to major general of the regular army, which was the highest grade then existing by law. Generals Sherman and McPherson received commissions as brigadier generals in the regular army. At this time, there was a general relaxation among the troops, as many officers and soldiers sought furloughs, leaves of absence, and discharges.[5]

In July 1863, General Sherman's troops were encamped along the Big Black River, about twenty miles east of Vicksburg. General Steele's first division was posted in an area around the railroad bridge. Future operations were not expected until the late autumn months. Supplies were abundant coming by rail into Vicksburg.[6]

Chapter Two

The Battle for Chattanooga

As General Sherman's troops encamped at the Big Black River, General Rosecrans was moving against General Bragg at Chattanooga, Tennessee. Fearing his supply line was endangered, General Bragg withdrew his army from Chattanooga and concentrated them at Lafayette. As Rosecrans pursued Bragg, he came under attack at Chickamauga on September 19. On September 19, due to misunderstanding and confusion, a gap was created in the Union lines by General Charles Wood. The Confederates poured through this gap, causing the Union line to collapse, leading to a rout of the Northern forces. Rosecrans's army pulled back to Chattanooga a few miles to the north, followed by the Confederate army. The demoralized Northern army was able to establish its defensive lines, and Bragg decided to put them into a state of siege. The army at Chattanooga had a difficult time procuring supplies, and a state of starvation had set in. General Sherman first got word of the impending disaster on September 22. He received orders from General Grant to go toward Chattanooga. Around this time, Sam's commander, General Frederick Steele of the First Division, Fifteenth Corps, Army of the Tennessee, was appointed to command the Department of Arkansas. General Peter J. Osterhaus was selected to command the First Division.

In his letter of September 13, 1863 from Black River, Mississippi, Samuel Heizer comments on the change in leadership:

> The commander of our Brigade, Col. Williamson of the 4th Iowa Infantry says we have fewer sick men and more men to die than any other regiment in the Brigade. Since General Osterhaus has taken command of our Division we have to drill more and be more particular in every respect than when Steele commanded. Guards must have their brass scoured their clothes neat and their shoes blackened when they appear have at Guard Mounting. We have already had Division Drill one day and Brigade Drill one day. We have inspection once a week by a staff officer and Sunday mornings by company commanders.
>
> Besides this we are required to drill two hours per day at 5 1/2 o'clock. So we are not idle always. We have a little to do Sundays. Inspection at 9:00 and drill parade in the evening.

On the same day (September 22), Sherman ordered the first Division to move toward Chattanooga. Sherman's troops were to repair the Memphis & Charleston Railroad as they moved toward Chattanooga. On October 2, Osterhaus's division had reached Corinth. Work on the railroad made progress slow.

Sam writes to his parents from Camp Wood, Mississippi, October 4, 1863: "We reached Corinth Wednesday evening and came to our present camp next day. We're about two miles and a half from Corinth on high piece of ground with good water convenient."

The Battle for Chattanooga

Near the middle of October, several command changes occurred. General Grant was placed in command of the Military Division of the Mississippi. This included the armies of the Cumberland, Ohio, and Tennessee. General Rosecrans, who was entrapped in Chattanooga, was replaced by General George H. Thomas. General Sherman, who was the commander of the XV Corps of the Army of the Tennessee was promoted to command the Department and Army of the Tennessee. General Frank P. Blair was temporarily given the command of the Fifteenth Corps.

Sherman's troops were still repairing railroad on October 27, when he received orders from Grant to proceed as quickly as possible to Bridgeport, about twenty-five miles west of Chattanooga. The Fifteenth Corps then marched to Eastport, where they crossed the Tennessee River. The troops marched to Elk River, which was crossed by ferry, then moving on to Elkton, Winchester, and Decherd. Sherman arrived in Bridgeport on November 13, followed by his troops. On the fourteenth, Sherman rode into Chattanooga, meeting with Grant and Thomas to survey the area and discuss plans for breaking the siege. General Joseph Hooker, in the meantime, had moved his Eleventh and Twelfth Corps from Bridgeport to Wauhatchee, which was about ten miles west of Chattanooga.

General Sherman returned to Bridgeport, where his troops were encamped. He then moved three of four divisions of his corps out by way of the main road. On the twentieth, Sherman reached General Hooker's headquarters just above Wauhatchee. At this time, the First Division of the Fifteenth Corps of the Army of the Tennessee was commanded by Peter J. Osterhaus. The First Division was made up of two brigades, led by Brigadier General C. R. Woods and Colonel J. A. Williamson of the Fourth Iowa. Sam's regiment, the Thirtieth Iowa, was part of Colonel Williamson's brigade. Sherman's troops were strung all the way from Bridgeport to Wauhatchee. Sam's division was bringing up the rear.

The plan called for Sherman to cross the Tennessee River by a pontoon bridge at Brown's Ferry, several miles downriver from Chattanooga. The troops would then encamp behind some hills, where the Confederates could not see them. Then, on the day of the attack, the troops would re-cross the Tennessee River near where Chickamauga Creek flows into it. This would put the troops north of Chattanooga on Missionary Ridge.

General Sherman in his *Memoirs*[7] makes these comments:

My command had marched from Memphis, 330 miles, and I had pushed them as fast as the roads and distance would admit, but I saw enough of the condition of man and animals in Chattanooga to inspire me with renewed energy.... No troops ever were or could be in better condition than mine, or who labored harder to fill their part.

In describing the crossing of the Tennessee River, Sherman says:

On the 21st I got the 2nd Division over Brown's Ferry Bridge and General Ewing got up; but the bridge broke repeatedly, and delays occurred which no human sagacity could prevent. All labored night and day, and General Ewing got over on the 23rd; but my rear division was cut off by the broken bridge at Brown's Ferry, and could not join me. I offered to go into action with my three divisions supported by General Jeff C. Davis, leading one of my best divisions (Osterhaus's) to act with General Hooker against Lookout Mountain. That division has not joined me yet, but I know and feel that it has served the country well, and that it has reflected honor on the Fifteenth Army Corps and the Army of the Tennessee. I leave the record of its history to General Hooker, or whomsoever has had its services during the late memorable events, confident that all will do it merited honor.

The Battle for Chattanooga

On November 24, 1863, General Hooker's troops, which included units from three different corps, were ready to move against Lookout Mountain and the narrow valley between the mountain and Missionary Ridge. Hooker's mission was to clear this valley of Confederate forces and take possession of Rossville Gap. He would then be in position to threaten the Confederate left and rear.

Brigadier General Peter J. Osterhaus commanded the First Division of Sherman's Fifteenth Corps, of which Sam Heizer was a member. About 8:00 AM, Hooker's troops began to move. Sam's division crossed Lookout Creek by a bridge about one and a half miles north of a ford used by General Geary. The report of the ensuing action of the Thirtieth Iowa Infantry is given by J. A. Williamson, Colonel, Fourth Iowa, commanding the Second Brigade, First Division:

HDQRS. SECOND BRIG., FIRST DIV. XV CORPS
Camp at Ringgold, Ga., Nov. 28, 1863

CAPTAIN: I have the honor to report the action of this brigade in the battles of Lookout Mountain, Missionary Ridge, and Ringgold; including all its movements from the 24th until the evening of the 27th instant.

The Brigade is composed of the 4th Iowa Infantry, commanded by Lt. Col. Burton; the 9th Iowa Infantry, commanded by Col. David Carskaddon; the 25th Iowa Infantry, commanded by Col. George A. Stone; the 26th Iowa Infantry, commanded by Col. Milo; the 30th Iowa Infantry, commanded by Lieut. Col. A. Roberts; and the 31st Iowa Infantry, commanded by Lt. Col. J. W. Jenkins. At the hour named in the order of the night previous the Brigade moved, following the 1st Brigade, to a point in front of Lookout Mountain, near where the attack was to be commenced, and formed line of battle by battalions en masse at deploying intervals. Very soon after my line was formed I received an order from you to send a regiment to support a battery on the hill immediately in front of Lookout Mountain, and commanding that portion of it when our troops were making the attack. I detached my right regiment, the Fourth, and sent it to the place designated. Soon after this I received another order to send one more regiment, to report to yourself, for some purpose of unknown to me. In obedience to the order, I sent you the Twenty-fifth. The four remaining regiments I held in line until about 11 o'clock, when I received an order from General Osterhaus to send another regiment to support a battery of Parrot guns immediately in our front. In obedience to this order, I sent the Thirtieth. I was then ordered to follow in the direction the 1st Brigade had taken with my three remaining regiments, which I did, until I arrived at the crossing of Lookout Creek, at which place Gen. Osterhaus ordered my rear regiment (the ninth) to remain and receive all the prisoners then there and those to be sent back. I crossed the creek with my two remaining regiments, when General Hooker in person sent another regiment (the Twenty-sixth) down the railroad to support some troops at a point or gap somewhere toward our left.

I then proceeded up the mountainside with my one remaining regiment (the Thirty-first), accompanied by Gen. Osterhaus in person, with a part of his staff, and came up with the 1st Brigade at a point where the troops not belonging to the 1st Division were in line, engaging the enemy. At this point I had some doubts as to where I should place my regiment on account of a dense fog which had settled down on the mountain side and prevented me from seeing the location of our troops, but soon found the line formed by a part of the 1st Brigade, and placed the regiment on the left of it. I was very soon joined by the Ninth and Twenty-sixth, which had been relieved and sent up to me, and placed them in line. At this place I learned from Gen. Osterhaus that the 4th Iowa had been sent forward early in the day, and that they were at that time somewhere up the mountain side; also that it had behaved well in the morning in driving the enemy from their breastworks. About 2 p.m. an aid-de-camp from Gen. Hooker ordered me to relieve a regiment of Gen. Geary's command, which was in the extreme front, under heavy fire and out of ammunition. I immediately sent my adjutant-general, Capt. George E. Ford, with the Thirty-first Regiment, to relieve the regiment, which was the ....

While my adjutant was there he found the 54 Ohio (?) also of Gen. Geary's command was out of ammunition, and relieved it with the 4th Iowa, which he found up at the front. After these regiments had been under fire, they sent me word that their ammunition was nearly exhausted. I immediately informed Gen. Osterhaus of the fact, and was informed by him that the Twenty-fifth and Thirtieth Regiments of my brigade, which had been left behind, must relieve them.

Captain Ford then started on foot in search of these regiments, but they had been ordered to different points, and could not be found, the captain returning after several hours' walk, nearly worn out by his unceasing exertion in the discharge of his duty.

In the meantime, before Capt. Ford returned, I applied to Gen. Geary, asking him to relieve my regiment, inasmuch as they had relieved his in the first instance. He refused to do it. I then took some ammunition from the remaining regiments with me to the regiments under fire, and afterward, about 1 a.m. went to General Geary and procured 8000 rounds of ammunition to replace what had been taken from my regiments. Soon after 2 a.m., the enemy having previously ceased firing and retreated, General Geary relieved the Fourth and Thirty-first regiments, and they fell back to their places in line of battle.

Early in the morning of the 25th, the Thirtieth and Twenty-fifth Regiments, having been relieved by Gen. Butterfield, of Gen. Hooker staff, reported to me, and took their positions in line, thus bringing my brigade together for the first time since the morning previous. About 9 o'clock on the morning of the 25th, my brigade was ordered to march toward Missionary Ridge. When we arrived near the pass where the enemy made the first stand, I received an order to take two regiments and ascend to hill in the left of the gap or pass. I accordingly took the Fourth and Thirty-first and pushed rapidly to the top, meeting with but little opposition. I pushed my skirmishers forward into the valley, where I expected to find the enemy, but they had gone. I remained on the top of the ridge for a short time, until the Ninth and Thirtieth Regiments came up (the Twenty-fifth and Twenty-sixth having been ordered by Gen. Osterhaus to take a take position on the western slope of the ridge to keep back any flanking force of the enemy which might come from our left), when I went forward to the valley, and then moved out by the flank, through the gap down the pass to the open ground, when I was ordered to make a short halt. While at the halt, two men of the 9th Iowa captured Lieut. Breckenridge, a son of Maj. Gen. John C. Breckenridge of the Confederate Army. In obedience to orders, I again proceeded up the main road by the right flank, still leaving the Twenty-fifth and Twenty-sixth in position which had been assigned them. The road on which I marched was up on a ridge east of and parallel with Missionary Ridge. I had not proceeded far before I heard heavy firing toward the front, on the left flank. I immediately ordered the Fourth Regiment detached, and deployed it as skirmishers on my left flank, and soon discovered that the enemy occupied that part of Missionary Ridge where I had been the short time before, and then moved by brigade forward, in line of battle, obliquely to the right, closing up on the first Brigade, at the same time bringing my left forward, in line with Gen. Cruft's division on my left. I then received orders from Gen. Osterhaus to go rapidly forward in line.

This movement was executed gallantly by the four regiments of the brigade present going down the side of the ridge we were then on and up the steep ascent of Missionary Ridge, all the time under heavy fire of the enemy, but driving them before us.

As I ascended the hill, I was in much doubt and perplexity as to whether I might not be inflicting severe injury on my own skirmishers, and also on the right of the division on my left.

This uncertainty kept me from reaching the summit as soon as I otherwise might have done; but, notwithstanding this, I think I may justly claim that one of my regiments (the Fourth) was the first to reach the top, and that the brigade was there as soon as any other troops.

I took a great number of prisoners, but could not state accurately how many, as I ordered them to be left behind under a very small guard, while the command pushed forward, and before I could ascertain the number they were turned over to the officer who seemed to be taking charge of all the prisoners. The brigade captured as large a number as did any other command.

Many instances of personal bravery might be mentioned, but it must be sufficient to say that all the regiments did well. Lt. W. M. Stimpson, of my staff (of the 30th Iowa Regiment), received a wound in the head in the beginning of the engagement, but continued to discharge his duties until the end. The brigade encamped on the field (here the Twenty-fifth and Twenty-sixth came up, having been relieved) and took care of our wounded, and buried our dead during the night. On the following morning, after picking up a large number of arms, delivering them to ordnance officer, I moved forward, following 1st Brigade, and encamped for the night four miles east of Chickamauga Creek.

On the morning of the 27th, the brigade marched at 5 o'clock toward Ringgold, where it arrived about 10 o'clock and found the enemy strongly posted on a range of hills, known as Taylor's Ridge, a short distance to the east of the town. Gen. Osterhaus ordered me to send one regiment to support the 76th Ohio of the 1st Brigade, which had been sent with a view to taking the hill. I immediately ordered the Fourth Regiment forward, instructing its commander to push forward and render all the assistance possible to the regiment in front, and then, in obedience to an order from Gen. Osterhaus, I brought forward and other regiment (the Thirty-first),and placed it along the railroad to act as sharpshooters, to cover the advance of the two regiments sent forward. Finding that the two regiments sent up were meeting with stubborn resistance, I took two other regiments (the Ninth and Twenty-sixth) and went forward with them in person, advancing up the side of the hill (which might be more properly called a mountain) until I came in line with the 4th Iowa and 76th Ohio on the left. In the meantime, before I could get two regiments (the Ninth and Twenty-sixth) up, the 4th Iowa and 76th Ohio had advanced to the top of the hill, but for want of support, after suffering severe loss, had been compelled to fall back a short distance (not more than 50 or 60 paces from the summit),where they were when I came up.

While I was gaining this position my two remaining regiments, the Twenty-fifth and Thirtieth, had in obedience to my order gone up to my left and were fast approaching the top, their skirmishers being not more than 75 paces from the summit, when three regiments (as I am informed of the XII Corps) came up, one on the left of the Twenty-fifth and one between the Twenty-fifth and Thirtieth, the other passing through the Twenty-fifth by the flank.

Col. Stone ordered and begged them to go up on his left, but the officers in command said they had orders for doing as they did, and persisted in their course. At this time the fire of the enemy had almost ceased, but they could be plainly seen making dispositions of their forces to repel the advance of the regiments. Col. Stone cautioned them that the enemy would open a destructive fire on them if they went up in the manner they were going. They replied they would teach "Western troops a lesson," and advanced a short distance farther, when the enemy opened a terrific fire on them. They stood manfully for a minute or two, when they gave way, and came down like an avalanche, carrying everything before them, and to the extent propagating the panic among my regiments. The fault of these regiments seemed to be more in the way in which they attempted to go up the hill than in anything else. While Col. Stone preferred the method of taking it by skirmishing cautiously advancing, the regiments above named tried to go up as if on parade where the men could barely have gone up by clinging to the rocks and bushes. Cols. Stone and Roberts did all they could to hold their men together, and soon succeeded in restoring order and confidence, and again went up the hill.

Having no support on the right, and those regiments on the left having given way in confusion, I found it would be folly to try to carry the hill until I should be reinforced, and accordingly made the best disposition of my force to hold the ground already gained, and sent a messenger to inform Gen. Osterhaus of the fact, and received from him an order to hold my position and await re-enforcements.

I held my position for a short time. No re-enforcements or support coming to my aid, and finding that the fire from the enemy had slackened, I again went forward and gained the top of the ridge and found the enemy retreating, and a strong force farther on burning the railroad bridge across the East Chickamauga Creek. I immediately went forward, keeping up a heavy fire, and drove them away before they accomplished in their work. I had the fire put out on the 1st Brigade, and sent Maj. Nichols of the 4th Iowa, and a small party of men, who volunteered for the service, to put out the fire on the bridge farther on. This he accomplished, after driving a much larger force than his own away. I cannot speak too highly of the conduct of Maj. Nichols throughout all the campaign, and especially in every action. First Lt. Charles W. Baker of Co. C and 2nd Lt. Thomas H. Cramer of Co. K, 4th Iowa, both distinguished themselves in the front of the fight, capturing prisoners from the very midst of the enemy. Lt. Cramer was instantly killed, after making a capture of a lieutenant and several men, and Lt. Baker mortally wounded (since dead) while heroically cheering the men on. Maj. Willard Warner, 76th Ohio, and his officers and men won my unqualified admiration. Many instances of heroic daring and bravery came under my observation, and would be reported specifically if regimental commanders had furnished me the names of the parties. Capt. George E. Ford, my assistant adjutant general, was severely wounded in the leg while trying to prevent the troops on my left from giving way, during the engagement at Ringgold. Lt. L. Shields, aid-de-camp, also received a slight wound in the hip at the same time. I am much indebted to my staff officers-- Capt. Ford, Capt. Darling, and Lts. Shields and Stimpson for their efficient services. Accompanying this report you will find list [not found] of killed and wounded of the several regiments in the different engagements.[8]

In his letter of December 2, 1863 to his sister, Sam describes his activities of the previous weeks. He said about a week earlier, he was feeling ill with the ague and wasn't feeling well enough to write home. Then he says:

>Since then I have been with the Company all the time. We have been in two fights since then. In both of these there were a good many killed and wounded. But I was not touched in either although in the last one the bullets came closer than I ever heard them before. David Carmean was laying just to my right behind the same log that I was, for the balls flew so thick and fast at us that we all lay behind logs, trees, stumps, and whatever else we could find and Dave said he saw splinters fly from the log nearly all the time. Now I know they came close to me for the log was scarcely as thick as my body. I thought certain my time had come at last. But the bullets kept flying and I was not touched. One Regiment close to ours lost all their officers but two in the 7th Ohio. Our Company was very fortunate. We had but one man touched and he was only scratched on his head enough to bring and numb his hand for two or three hours. Our two fights were on Mission Ridge, Tennessee and White Oak Ridge, Georgia. We did not get to fight at Lookout Mountain because they put us on a little hill to guard a battery that was throwing shells at the rebels. We had a good view of the fight. We could see the rebels running and our men running after them.

We felt very glad when we saw our men driving them. They kept us beside the battery all day then ordered us up the mountain. It did not seem very far up. But we had to stop three or four times to rest before we got to the top. The mountain is nearly one-half mile high. But I must end in a hurry for it is getting late and cold.

I believe the boys are all well except Newton McBride and William Darlington. They are both with the company. The rebels are driven from this part of the country and we expect to start for Huntsville tomorrow.

On December 31, 1863, Sam was encamped at Woodville, Alabama. The weather was rainy, cold, and unpleasant. Sam had been in command of Company F, filling in since the regiment had left Bridgeport.

January 9, 1864 found Sam encamped at Paint Rock River, Alabama. The weather was cold, but the men had built warm shelters. On January 28, 1864, Sam was still at Paint Rock River, but the weather was much improved, *like spring in Iowa,* he says. Sam wrote on February 4, 1864 that they were laying idle in camp and were unemployed except for guard duty as well as scouting or foraging parties. He mentioned that the scouting party carried Springfield Rifled Muskets.

In his letter to his parents on February 7, 1864, Sam told about Lt. Col. Roberts of his regiment, who led a detail guarding the Tennessee River for about twenty miles. The soldiers were watching some rebels across the river. It was reported that the Union soldiers made a crossing of the river to engage the enemy near Guntersville, Alabama.

Sam's letter of February 14, 1864 reports that they are holding several rebel prisoners there. In his letter of the twenty-second of February, the regiment was still at Paint Rock Creek, Alabama. This was Sam's birthday. He was twenty-two years old. He mentioned General Osterhaus was with them again and everyone was glad to see him.

On May 1, 1864, Sam was at Woodville, Alabama. A week earlier, his regiment marched to Trianna, Alabama by way of Huntsville, Alabama. After several days, they were ordered back to Woodville. Upon arriving at Woodville, they discovered that their division had left for Chattanooga. He thought the division would be guarding the railroad between Stevenson and Chattanooga.

Chapter Three

The March to Atlanta

On March 18, 1864, Major General Sherman assumed command of the Military Division of the Mississippi. His armies included the Army of the Ohio, commanded by General John Schofield, the Army of the Cumberland, commanded by General George Thomas, and the Army of the Tennessee, commanded by General James B. McPherson. General John A. Logan was in command of the Fifteenth Army Corps of the Army of the Tennessee.[9]

By the first week of May, Sherman's army was ready to move toward Atlanta, Georgia. On the first of May, General McPherson brought his troops quickly to Chattanooga. Some troops came by rail, others by marching. By May 4, McPherson was moving troops into Chattanooga and spreading toward Gordon's Mill. On May 7, General Thomas moved against Tunnel Hill near Ringgold, Georgia. Tunnel Hill was lightly guarded and easily taken. From Tunnel Hill, Buzzard's Roost or Mill Creek Gap could be seen, where many of the enemy were visible, ready to defend this narrow passageway through the mountains. The Confederate position was too strong for a concerted attack. General Sherman had Thomas and Schofield press the front, while General McPherson marched farther to the west through a little-known and undefended gap called Snake Creek Gap. McPherson emerged from the gap behind the enemy near Resaca on May 9. McPherson thought the Confederate position too strong and failed to attack. He then retreated to the mouth of Snake Creek Gap. General Sherman gently reproved McPherson, telling him he had missed an opportunity that might only come once in a lifetime. Sherman said, "He had in hand twenty-three thousand of the best men in the army, and could have walked into Resaca (then held only by a small brigade)..."[10]

The major part of the army was moved southward through Snake Creek Gap on the twelfth and thirteenth of May. On the fourteenth, the army closed in on Resaca on the north and west side. On the fifteenth, there was continuous battle and skirmishing. Toward evening on the fifteenth, McPherson—with his whole line of battle—took a ridge overlooking Resaca, where his field artillery could carry a railroad bridge that crossed the Oostenaula River. His army repulsed several sallies that attempted to drive him from his position. The night of the fifteenth, General Joe Johnston evacuated Resaca across the Oostenaula River. On May 20, 1864, Sam writes to his parents about the battle of Resaca:

> As I have a chance to write this morning I thought it would be well to let you know I'm not dead, wounded or taken prisoner although I have been pretty badly scared. I was in a fight at Resaca three days. On the evening of the second day, May 14, we charged nearly a half-mile and drove the enemy about a quarter. So you see we are now at Kingston.

General Sherman's army was now in pursuit. General McPherson crossed the Oostenaula River at Lay's Ferry by pontoon bridge, which was earlier put in place. The army reached Kingston on the nineteenth. McPherson's head of column was then about four miles west of the place known as Woodlawn. He was then ordered to continue marching on roads south of Kingston, heading toward Cassville. On May 20, the Confederates had left Cassville. On the twenty-third, the army began its march, heading to Marietta by way of Dallas. McPherson's army was placed on the right side of General Thomas's army. Sherman's army crossed the Etowah River, heading south toward Dallas. On the twenty-fifth, McPherson was on the right, near Van Wert. Geary's division of Hooker's Twentieth Corps drove off rebel cavalry near Pumpkin Vine Creek. As he followed the cavalry near the Altoona-to-Dallas road, he hit a heavy force of infantry, and a battle developed. This engagement occurred near New Hope Church.[11]

On May 26, McPherson had reached Dallas and had put his troops on the east and southeast of town. Being three miles from Hooker's troops, Sherman ordered McPherson to close the gap. On the twenty-eighth, McPherson began his movement and was met by a heavy force. After a bloody battle, he was able to withdraw on June 1 to join up with Hooker's forces at New Hope. On June 4, Sherman was preparing to withdraw, when General Johnston evacuated his position. On June 4, McPherson's Fifteenth Corps was moved to the extreme left.

The army on June 10 moved six miles to Big Shanty, where the enemy's position could be observed on three hills known as Lost Mountain, Pine Mountain, and Kennesaw Mountain. General Johnston had entrenched his 60,000 troops carefully in strongly fortified positions. McPherson's forces were on the left, which followed the railroad that curved around the north base of Kennesaw. On the fourteenth of June, Sherman's forces occupied lines ten miles long facing Kennesaw, Pine, and Lost Mountain. That day, Confederate General Polk was killed by an artillery volley on Pine Mountain while observing Union movements. On the fifteenth, Union lines advanced and found Pine Mountain to be abandoned. On the sixteenth, Lost Mountain was found abandoned by the Confederates. On the seventeenth and eighteenth, the rain was so heavy, operations were not possible.¹²

The date of June 27 was picked as the day to attack the enemy positions. The attack was begun at 9 AM. McPherson's forces fought up the face of lesser Kennesaw but were unable to reach the summit. By 11:30, the assault was over and had failed. McPherson had lost several valuable officers and five hundred men. McPherson was then moved to the extreme right back of General Thomas. Kennesaw was about fifteen miles north of the Chattahoochee River. Deciding to maneuver rather than attacking entrenched forces, Sherman moved his army to within three miles of the Chattahoochee River, in reach of the railroads. On the night of July 2, McPherson withdrew from his lines and moved along Nickajack Creek to the rear of Thomas's army. General Johnston then withdrew from Kennesaw and Marietta. Sherman then pursued Johnston, hoping to catch him as he crossed the Chattahoochee River. General Johnston had previous to this time prepared strong fortifications on the west side of the Chattahoochee River. McPherson's forces had reached the Chattahoochee below Turner's Ferry. When Sherman stood on a hill near Vining's Station near the Chattahoochee River, he could see buildings in Atlanta, nine miles distant. On July 5, it appeared that Johnston had the bulk of his army across the river. McPherson, on July 6, was on the right, where he made a demonstration near Turner's Ferry.¹³ On July 7, Sam wrote to his parents: "... We are now near the Chattahoochee River. The enemy it appears are nearly all across the river and what remains are getting across as fast as possible. Our company has had but two wounded since I wrote last ...."

Near July 9, Johnston moved his army across the Chattahoochee at Roswell, putting him on the extreme left of the army.

The general movement toward Atlanta began on July 17, 1864. McPherson's corps proceeded toward Stone Mountain. On the eighteenth, McPherson was marching between Stone

Mountain and Decatur. McPherson's advance guard reached Decatur about nightfall, where he met General Schofield's troops, who had already arrived. On this day, Sherman learned that General Joe Johnston had relinquished his command to General John Bell Hood. By July 19, the three armies were moving toward Atlanta with little resistance. McPherson was moving along the railroad near Decatur.[14]

Chapter Four

The Battle for Atlanta

The Battle of Peachtree Creek was fought on July 20. The Confederates attacked General Thomas's right with a major thrust against Hooker's Twentieth Corps. The attack occurred after noontime. The hard and close fighting went on for a couple of hours before the rebels retired from the field.

On July 22, the army was pressing for Atlanta. Sherman was near the Howard House when McPherson and his staff arrived. They went to the Howard House to discuss the movement of troops in General Dodge's Sixteenth Corps and General Giles A. Smith's Seventeenth Corps. During their discussion, some gunfire was unexpectedly heard toward Decatur. McPherson was sent to see what the firing was about. He took four of his staff with him. Shortly after McPherson had left, one of his staff hurriedly returned, saying McPherson was captured or killed. As it turned out, on the ride, McPherson had directed two of his staff to take messages requesting support of reserve brigades of the Fifteenth Corps. McPherson then rode into a group of Confederates, who demanded he surrender. McPherson, however, tried to ride to safety and was shot by the

Confederate soldiers. Sherman then sent for John A. Logan, the commanding officer of the Fifteenth Corps, who immediately assumed command of the Army of the Tennessee.[15]

Confederate General Hood, on the night of the twenty-first, had sent his troops to Decatur to get behind McPherson's lines. McPherson's cavalry had been sent on a mission and was not present to guard McPherson's flank. Under the cover of forest, the Confederates were able to get close to the Union troops undetected. General Dodge's troops (the Sixteenth Corps) had been at Decatur and were moving in support of McPherson near Atlanta. The Confederates struck Dodge's troops, but were driven back. About this time, the Confederates struck Giles A. Smith's troops and pushed them back toward Leggett's Division (Seventeenth Corps) near a hill. Here a bloody battle raged from just after noon until after nightfall.[16]

General Charles R. Woods's First Division of the Fifteenth Corps (Sam's division) was on the extreme right of the Army of the Tennessee. They were closed up with General Scofield's troops. Woods's troops had been swept back and had lost connection with General Logan's troops on Leggett's Hill. Sherman ordered Woods's troops to wheel left to catch the enemy in flank. General Schofield brought up gun batteries, which hurled shells over the heads of Woods's division in their support. The troops advanced, regaining a parapet which had been lost earlier. At the same time, General Logan rallied a division that had been along the railroad and regained ground that had been lost. These two forces combined and drove the Confederates back into Atlanta. This battle of July 22 is known as the Battle of Atlanta. Sherman said of this battle:

> I purposely allowed the Army of the Tennessee to fight this battle almost unaided save by demonstrations on the part of General Schofield and Thomas against the fortified lines to their immediate fronts, and by detaching as described, one of Schofield's brigades to Decatur, because I knew that the attacking force could

only be a part of Hood's army, and that, if any assistance were rendered by either of the armies, the Army of the Tennessee would be jealous. Nobly did they do their work that day, and terrible was the slaughter done to our enemy, though at sad cost to ourselves....[17]

It was at this time, July 24, that a new commanding general was chosen to direct the Army of the Tennessee. General O. O. Howard was chosen to replace General John Logan, who had been temporarily in command after General James B. McPherson had been killed on the twenty-second of July. General Logan became commander of the Fifteenth Corps.[18]

EZRA CHURCH

From their lines after the Battle of Atlanta, Sherman planned to send the Army of the Tennessee to the right, behind the other Union armies, to move west and southward toward the railroad south of Atlanta. The movement began on July 27. By evening, the Sixteenth Corps was in position at Proctor's Creek. The next morning, the Fifteenth Corps arrived and joined Blair's Seventeenth Corps. Their location was near a meeting hall called Ezra Church. Confederate General Hood had detected the Union movement and had sent General S. D. Lee with General Stewart in reserve, to intercept the Union forces. When he arrived, he found the Army of the Tennessee entrenched and ready for battle. By 11:30 AM, a severe battle had begun. The Confederates, surprised to find the Union troops already in place, attacked immediately. Their attacking thrusts lacked coordination and order. As waves of Confederate troops assaulted the Federal lines, they were thrown back with great loss. General Howard had placed his artillery so that he could rain shells on the attackers. General Howard, who had been with the Army of the Tennessee in every battle since First Manassas in 1861, said he had never seen fighting like this before. The battle continued until about

4 PM, with great loss to the Confederate forces. General Logan (Fifteenth Corps) in his report said the worst fighting fell on generals Harrow and Morgan L. Smith's fronts, but that these and Brigadier General C. R. Woods are entitled to equal credit for gallantry and skill in the battle. Major generals Blair and Dodge also gave assistance when needed. The Confederates had lost about 5,000 men, which included four wounded generals. The Union had lost fewer than 700 men. At this time, the Army of the Tennessee consisted of the Fifteenth, Sixteenth, and Seventeenth Corps.[19]

Samuel Heizer wrote to his sister Irene on August 5, 1864, "In that Field before Atlanta, Georgia." He writes:

> Since I wrote to you last I have been in several fights. But so far I have not been touched by the rebs. I hope I shall be as fortunate in the future, and get to see home once more. We are now lying in reserve in the second line of breastworks. Our duty is very light. We have no skirmishing to do. The last time we had any duty to do we were on picket in the rear. We did not see any rebels and I think there were none there. But then we have to look out for them in every direction so as not to let them come up when we are not looking for them and capture some of us or some of our rations or destroy the railroad behind us.
>
> There has been some pretty hard fighting in this neighborhood lately but we have been fortunate enough not to be present at any of it since the 28th of July. That day we had the one-man hurt slightly. Our regiment has been very fortunate since we left Kennesaw Mountain. We have had but three severely wounded during the last month."

At the end of Sam's letter he told Irene, "You may call me Capt. Sam B. Heizer," announcing his promotion. Sam was now twenty-two years old.

The Battle for Atlanta

JONESBORO

The month of July had been very hot. The fighting had been constant, and four major battles had occurred, with the casualties in the thousands. August began hot and sultry. Progress was slow with the process of the siege. The men did not have a lot to do, many loitering in the trenches. The railroad moving south from Atlanta toward Macon was the one supply line that kept Atlanta in Confederate hands. Control of this railroad line would mean the fall of Atlanta. Atlanta, known as the "Gate-City of the South," was full of machine shops, arsenals, and foundries. Taking Atlanta could cripple the Confederacy.[20]

General Sherman decided to step up the shelling of Atlanta. He ordered two thirty-pound Parrotts from Chattanooga with which he could level almost any building in Atlanta. By August 10, the Parrotts were in position, and a sharp and heavy fire was directed toward Atlanta.[21]

On August 17, 1864, Sam wrote to his parents from a half mile in the rear of his regiment, the Thirtieth Iowa. He said:

> As you see I am not on duty with the regiment. For several days I have been troubled with a severe headache caused Dr. Rogers says by being overheated last summer while in the Vicksburg campaign. I got permission of the Colonel and Dr. to go to the rear to where the doctor says for a few days to see if rest and quiet would not stop my complaint. I came out yesterday in the forenoon. My head troubles me but very little when I keep cool and quiet; but heat or noise give me great pain and sometimes it seems as if my head would burst. In other respects I am quite well. I hope that a week's rest will be of great advantage to me. If I do not get better by that time I think very likely I will go to a hospital where I can get more attention. Since I wrote home last Company C has had but one man killed and one wounded. Our rifle pits until a few days ago were in plain view of the rebel's skirmish pits

at a distance of about 150 yards. Both these men were shot in our rifle pits. John W. Howell was wounded by a ball striking along our breastworks and glancing. E. T. Huleing was shot across the back near the kidneys while digging in our rifle pit and died almost instantly. Co. B's first lieutenant was shot through the head by a stray ball the other day and died a short time after. Besides these there have been four in the regiment wounded during the last week or two. ... Our company has been unfortunate during the campaign thus far. We started from Paint Rock with 34 men and have lost 13 (11 wounded and two killed); over one-third of the number we started with."

Eight days later, August 25, 1864, Sam wrote to his parents and brother:

Our regiment I have just heard is under marching orders and I cannot write much. I wrote so short note that time ago that I have but little news. I have improved in health and I'm going back to the regiment this evening. We are now again on the second line; our skirmishers have driven back the rebel skirmishers and the second Brigade of our division having thrown up a line of works in our front, which we now occupy. I am expecting a lively time shortly. Everything seems to indicate a movement of great importance.

On the twenty-fourth, General Sherman was preparing for a movement of his army. He telegraphed General Halleck that Atlanta was experiencing heavy fires caused by Union artillery fire. He said he would move his army around Atlanta by the south on the following night and would have enough provisions for his army to last for twenty days.

General Dodge of the Sixteenth Corps had been wounded in the head and had been sent to the rear. His two divisions were divided between the Fifteenth and the Seventeenth Corps. The operation started on the evening of the twenty-fifth, as

The Battle for Atlanta

expected, with the movement of several corps. The evening of the twenty-sixth, the Fifteenth and Seventeenth Corps of the Army of the Tennessee moved out and made a wide circuit to the extreme right. The movement of the troops caused those in Atlanta to think the Union forces had withdrawn in retreat. On August 28, General Thomas and General Howard reached the West Point Railway, which they proceeded to break up on the twenty-ninth. On the thirtieth, Howard's forces were headed for Jonesboro. Upon reaching Jonesboro on the thirty-first, Howard found Hardee's corps entrenched. Howard's men immediately began to dig rifle pits. The rebels came out to meet the Fifteenth Corps about 3 PM and were easily driven back. Davis's Fourteenth Corps, who had been tearing up railroad, marched for Jonesboro on September 1. Davis came into line on his right with Howard's corps. After getting his divisions into line about 4 PM, Davis's corps swept over the rebel parapet, capturing all of Govan's Brigade along with two field batteries of ten guns.

Also captured in this assault were members of Kentucky's Orphan Brigade, including Johnny Green, about whom a book has been written. As night came on, Hardee's corps escaped.[22]

The next morning, as Sherman pursued Hardee near Lovejoy's Station, he learned that Atlanta had been evacuated and that General Slocum was in the city. When the word got out, there was great joy and laughter among the troops. Soon President Lincoln got the unexpected news: "Atlanta is ours, and fairly won." This news helped Lincoln get re-elected in the November election of 1864.

On September 5, the three Union armies were assigned places to camp. The Army of the Tennessee was placed at East Point, which is located south of Atlanta, between Atlanta and Jonesboro. Sherman rode into Atlanta on September 8, which was occupied by General Slocum's Twentieth Corps. Sherman issued orders to evacuate all citizens and families from Atlanta, to make the city purely a military garrison.

Shortly after the fall of Atlanta, generals Blair (Twentieth Corps) and Logan (Fifteenth Corps) left for home to take care of politics. These generals were volunteers and not of the regular army. On September 15, Hood's army was still in the area of Lovejoy's Station, south of Jonesboro. By September 15, things had settled down. Many of the regiments had reached their expiration-of-service date and were on the way home.[23] On September 15, Sam wrote a letter home from East Point. He discusses mostly family concerns but says: "We had inspection of everything today. The inspecting officer gave us great praise for our industry. He said we have the best kept guns in the Brigade."

THE PURSUIT OF HOOD

It seems that about this time, Sam returned home on furlough. In the meantime, General Hood began to move his troops from Lovejoy's Station to the west side of the Chattahoochee River. General Sherman's army had gone through some changes. General Schofield had gone to the rear. General Thomas was sent to Chattanooga with two divisions. The Army of the Tennessee was still commanded by Major General O. O. Howard, but the Fifteenth Corps was now commanded by Major General Osterhaus, and the Seventeenth Corps by Major General T. E. G. Ransom.[24]

Hood's army was traveling northward, threatening the railway and communications. On the third and fourth of October, he crossed the Chattahoochee River, and the next day was at Marietta and Kennesaw. The Confederates made a determined attack on Altoona on the fifth, and a desperate battle ensued, where General Corse of the Fourth Division of the Fifteenth Corps was able to hold off the enemy. By 4 PM the battle was over.[25]

The rebels appeared near Rome on October 10. On the eleventh, General Corse at Rome reported that the enemy had disappeared. On the twelfth, Sherman at Rome learned that

The Battle for Atlanta

Hood turned up at Resaca and demanded its surrender. The garrison commander refused to surrender. Sherman had, at this time, dispatched cavalry to reinforce the garrison, and marched his army to Resaca, arriving during the night. The next morning, it was found that Hood's whole army had passed by, heading for Dalton. Hood's forces would destroy railroad as they moved. During the morning of the sixteenth, General Charles R. Woods's leading division took Ships Gap, and captured prisoners from a Southern regiment left there to hold back the Union movement. At Ship's Gap, Sherman heard from General Schofield that he was in Chattanooga but trying to reach Sherman's army. General Schofield finally reached Sherman at Gaylesville around October 21.[26]

Sam wrote to his parents from Chattanooga on October 18, 1864:

> As you see I have not yet reached the regiment. It seems very uncertain when I will be able to do it. I reached this place October 10 and the next day got on a train going south supposing I would be able to join the regiment in 24 hours, but upon arriving at Dalton we learned that the rebels had attacked Resaca and that it would be unsafe to proceed further. So the train backed up to Dalton where we remained until the next day when General Schofield came down from Knoxville and learning that the rebels were advancing on the place he ordered the three trains in the place back to Cleveland, Tennessee and from there back to Chattanooga where we arrived next morning. We got away from Dalton just in time for as soon as we left the enemy came into town and the garrison surrendered and as we were unarmed we would've been unable to render any aide to the garrison. Upon our arrival in Chattanooga the first commander Col. Stanley ordered all officers absent from their commands in the city not on duty here to report to headquarters and there gave orders to organize all the troops in the same situation as ourselves and

Col. Roberts was assigned to the commander of this detachment. I acted adjutant for the Col. until he was able to get a suitable lieutenant and now I have nothing to do. We are all longing to get to our regiments. There are several officers and men here of my acquaintance four of my own regiment so that I do not lack company. I have been in excellent health since leaving home. Have not heard from the regiment since I left it.

Six days later, on October 24, Sam wrote home from Chattanooga:

I have as yet been unable to join my regiment and am still on duty in this camp. I have however heard from the regiment two or three times. When I heard last all of my company were well. The regiment had not been in a fight since I left and from what I can learn I think they will not be in as much as Hood seems to be trying to make his escape southward and is now probably farther south than our army is prepared to follow him. I do not think Sherman can follow him very far because his teams are so worn out that they can do but little and without provisions an army can do nothing but starve and provisions sufficient to subsist an army are not to be found in the country after Hood's army has passed through. Rumors as to the destination of the Army of the Tennessee are very conflicting so that an opinion can hardly be formed and would be worthless when formed. So I shall not tell you when or where I will join my command simply because I have no idea when or where I will be able to join it. I am very anxious to get to the old 30th and shall attempt to get to it as soon as I think it worthwhile to try. I have not heard from home since Col. Roberts left and do not expect to till I reach the regiment.

The Battle for Atlanta

In the letter, Sam then goes on to say that he took a walk a few days earlier with captains Smith and Watkins and a captain from the Thirty-first Iowa. After getting a pass from General Steedman to go beyond the pickets, they made their way to Lookout Mountain. They went over part of the ground where the Battle of Lookout Mountain had taken place the previous autumn. Upon reaching the summit facing Chattanooga, he looked across the Chattanooga Valley and writes:

> Beyond that is Mission Ridge where last fall from our present position could be seen through a spyglass the vast armies of Grant and Bragg in deadly conflict. On the right center is Chattanooga with its government depots and workshops. In front is the Tennessee River winding among the mountains and hills. It seems as if nature had tried to hinder its progress by throwing mountains in its way. Yet it manages to pass all these and is lost in the far west behind mountains and still flows on. To our left is Lookout Valley and the creek of the same name. Beyond this creek the 15th Corps last autumn found Gen. Hooker fortified on a range of hills running parallel with Lookout Mountain. Beneath our feet around the side of the mountain Hooker's 11th and 12th Corps reinforced by Osterhaus's Division of the 15th Corps swept and the rebels fled in confusion like clouds before the wind. And I heard and joined in the shouts of the victors and heard the groans of the wounded and dying.

On October 19, General Sherman was busy setting up his plan to march through Georgia to the sea at Savannah. In a telegraphed message, he said the railroad was almost prepared near Big Shanty and should be finished in about ten days near Dalton. In another message, he said he would prepare Atlanta for evacuation to move through Georgia to the sea. On October 21, Sherman was in Gaylesville and remained there until the twenty-eighth. General Schofield arrived with two divisions, along with several generals. While at Gaylesville, Sherman's pursuit of Hood ceased.

At this time, the Fifteenth Corps was commanded by Peter J. Osterhaus in the absence of General John A. Logan.[27]

Sam was at Kingston, Georgia on October 27, and wrote to his parents:

> I have not yet reached the regiment and will not probably for about three days yet. Our battalion was detailed to guard a corps of Paymasters to Atlanta. We left Chattanooga Tuesday morning on the train and reached Dalton in the evening. Lay in the railroad depot overnight. Left Dalton about eight next morning and marched to Resaca.
>
> The railroad between Dalton and Tilton was not rebuilt. I understood that five miles were yet to be built. That I guess will be completed today. This morning we got on the cars at Resaca and reached Kingston about noon. Here Col. Roberts kindly relieved me and my lieutenant and consented to let us go on to the regiment while he and the battalion went on to Atlanta."...

In a telegram of November 2, 1864, Grant for the first time gave his consent for Sherman's proposed march to the sea.[28]

General Sherman was at Kingston on November 2. His four corps (the Fifteenth, Seventeenth, Fourteenth, and the Twentieth) were strung out from Rome to Atlanta. General Frank P. Blair had rejoined his corps, the Seventeenth.

Chapter Five

The March to The Sea

On the tenth of November, all of the troops who were to go on the campaign were ordered to move toward Atlanta. The movement to the sea had begun.

In Sam's letter of December 18, 1864, he told his parents:

I reached the regiment from home on the 31st day of October, just 28 days after leaving you. I was then at Cave Springs 16 miles from Rome. From there we went to Vinings Station 14 miles north of Atlanta. On Saturday Nov. 12 we were engaged destroying railroad northward thus cutting us off from all our friends and all supplies except what we had with us. The next day we began the march southward and resting one day near Atlanta proceeded on our way toward Macon.

The telegraph and railroad connections were broken with the rear on November 12. All the troops had arrived around Atlanta by November 14. Major General O. O. Howard was on the right wing, and Major General H. W. Slocum was on the left. The right wing was made up of the Fifteenth Corps of Major General Peter J. Osterhaus and the Seventeenth Corps of Major General Frank P. Blair.

The Fifteenth Corps was composed of four divisions. The divisions were commanded by brigadier generals Charles R. Woods (Sam's division), W. B. Hazen, John E. Smith, and John M. Corse.

The army was made up of the following army corps: the Fifteenth, Seventeenth, Fourteenth, and Twentieth, which were supported by Kilpatrick's Cavalry. The strength of the army totaled 59,545 men (November 10).

Great effort was given to take experienced, able-bodied soldiers who were well-armed. Having cut themselves off from supplies, the things they needed were packed onto wagons as much as possible. What they couldn't take along would be taken from the country they were moving through. The army planned to march about fifteen miles a day. Houses, mills, and cotton gins would be destroyed along the way. The army took 1,200,000 rations, which were to last for about twenty days. They also took a good supply of cattle to be driven along.[29]

On the morning of November 15, the right wing with cavalry marched out of Atlanta, following the railroad toward Jonesboro. The immediate intended destination was Milledgeville, which was the capital of Georgia at that time. The troops were to reach Milledgeville in about seven days, a distance of about 100 miles.

As General Sherman left Atlanta, he reflected on his experience in Atlanta in his *Memoirs*, (Volume 2, 178-179):

> About 7 AM of November 16th we rode out of Atlanta by the Decatur road, filled by marching troops and wagons of the Fourteenth Corps; and reaching the hill, just outside of the old rebel works, we naturally paused to look back upon the scenes of our past battles. We stood upon the very ground whereon was fought the bloody battle of July 22nd, and could see the copse of wood where McPherson fell. Behind us lay Atlanta, smoldering and in ruins, the black smoke rising high

The March to The Sea

in air, and hanging like a pall over the ruined city. A way off in the distance, on the McDonough road, was the rear of Howard's column, the gun-barrels glistening in the sun, the white-topped wagons stretching away to the south; and right before us the Fourteenth Corps, marching steadily and rapidly, with a cheery look and a swinging pace, that made light of the thousand miles that lay between us and Richmond. Some band, by accident, struck up the anthem of "John Brown's soul goes marching on"; the men caught up the strain, and never before or since have I heard the chorus of "Glory, glory, hallelujah!" done with more spirit, or in better harmony of time and place. Then we turned our horses' heads to the east; Atlanta was soon lost behind the screen of trees, and became a thing of the past. Around it clings many a thought of desperate battle, of hope and fear, that now seem like the memory of a dream; and I have never seen the place since. [30]

As the army moved forward, railroad would be torn up and the rails heated and twisted to make them unusable. Foraging parties were very active and brought in an abundance of food.

On November 23, Sherman rode into Milledgeville, the state capital. The Twentieth Corps was already there. Shortly after, General Howard wrote that after leaving Atlanta, he traveled toward Macon by two roads through Jonesboro and the McDonough. At Planters' Factory, he crossed the Ocmulgee River by a pontoon bridge on November 18 and 19. Howard then marched to Gordon by way of Monticello. Osterhaus's Fifteenth Corps was sent to support Kilpatrick's Cavalry in a feint on Macon. About four miles from Macon, Confederate cavalry came out and attacked Kilpatrick, who drove them back into their defenses. After charging and getting inside the enemy parapet, Kilpatrick was forced to return to his infantry support near Griswold Station. At Griswold, the Fifteenth

Corps tore up railroad eastward. Charles R. Woods's division was left here as a rear guard. One brigade, Walcott's, was entrenched across the road with some of Kilpatrick's Cavalry. On November 22, a division of troops under Confederate General G. W. Smith came out of Macon and attacked Walcutt's brigade. Smith's division was driven back into Macon by Walcutt's troops, who were armed with Spencer repeating rifles. The fire was so intense that Smith thought he was up against a whole division.[31]

The right wing continued to tear up railroad as they moved toward Savannah. When they reached the Oconee River, the right wing met some weak resistance, but was soon able to cross over by pontoon bridge. On the twenty-fourth, Sherman with the Twentieth Corps rode into Sandersville. On the twenty-seventh, Sherman rode to Tenille, six miles south of Sandersville, and found the railroad being destroyed by General Corse's division of the Fifteenth Corps. That day, Sam saw Sherman for the first time on this march.[32]

Writing to his parents on December 18 near Savannah, Sam describes some of the previously mentioned events:

> On the evening of November 21st we reached the Macon and Savannah railroad rear. Resting here the next day the rebels attacked the 2nd Brigade of our division and were driven back with a loss of about 1000 killed, wounded and prisoners. The 2nd Brigade lost but a few. The next day November 23rd we set out for Savannah. On Saturday November 26 we crossed the Oconee River. Sunday November 27 our Brigade destroyed nearly three miles of railroad and marched about 25 miles the hardest days work of the campaign. This day for the first time on the campaign I saw General Sherman. He had on a Colonel's coat without shoulder straps and was talking with another man by the roadside near his headquarters.

The March to The Sea

After Tenille station, the fifteenth Corps followed a road eastward that was south of the railroad.

Sherman entered Millen on December 3 with the Seventeenth Corps. General Howard with the Fifteenth Corps was south of the Ogeechee River opposite Scarborough, which was about five miles south of Millen. After destroying the depot and some other facilities in Millen, the march continued to Savannah. On December 5, the army was fifty miles from Savannah, near the Ogeechee Church. There, some fresh earthworks had been constructed by McLaw's Confederate division. McLaw, seeing his flanks were being turned, retreated into Savannah. Everything, including the weather, seemed to be going well. General Sherman comments: "Never do I recall a more agreeable sensation than the sight of our camps by night, lit up by the fires of fragrant pine-knots. The trains were all in good order, and the men seemed to march their 15 miles a day as though it were nothing."[33]

Sherman was eight miles from Savannah on December 8, at Pooler's Station. On the ninth and tenth, several corps had reached the defenses of the city. The Fifteenth Corps was on the extreme right. At this point, the city was completely invested. On inspecting the city's defenses, Sherman found them to be strong, and decided on a siege. The Confederates at Savannah were commanded by General William J. Hardee.

General Sherman made contact with the fleet in Ossabaw Sound and sent Howard's engineers to repair King's Bridge. On the evening of the twelfth, Sherman rode to a Mr. King's house, where he met with General Howard and General Hazen of the second division of the Fifteenth Army Corps. The next morning, General Hazen's troops passed over the bridge with orders to march down the right bank of the Ogeechee and take Fort McAllister by storm. The Second Division was the same one Sherman had commanded at Shiloh and Vicksburg. He had special confidence and pride in this unit. As the sun was declining, General Hazen attacked and took Fort McAllister.[34]

Sam continued in his letter of December 18 near Savannah:

From this time on we passed through pine forests and swamps making fifteen miles per day passing down the right side of the Ogeechee River to Wright Bridge where on the seventh of December our Brigade crossed and moved out to the railroad three miles where we met the 4th Division under General Corse. This day the 4th Division had a skirmish with the rebs and one skirmisher captured one Rebel with a blue coat on which Col. Williamson of the 4th Iowa commanding our Brigade made him exchange with a Negro for a gray jacket. Bully for him. If the soldiers had been permitted they would have killed him on the spot. This night as our wagons and pack mules were left on the other side of the river we were a little short of rations I have now. But some of the boys gave me my supper and the next morning our pack mules were up again. That night while posting pickets, I was Brigade Officer of the day I in company with the Officer of the day before with a guard just relieved summoned a squad of about 50 Gamblers. But as the guard was insufficient most of them escaped. What we still held we turned over to Brigade Headquarters where they were put under guard and sent to the commanding officers of the regiments to be disposed of by them as they thought best. Gambling has become very common among soldiers since they were paid off at Vinings Station and the evil has become so great that General Woods commanding our Division has ordered that all men found gambling shall have their money appropriated to the hospital fund and themselves and all who were even looking on whether engaged in the game or not put to work on the fortifications under fire of the enemy. I hope this order may have the desired effect. But to continue my story. We crossed the Ogeechee and marched down the west side to the mouth of the canal running to Savannah and 16 miles from the place. Here we crossed the river and marched out on the towpath of the canal to within about six miles of the city. Since there we have moved around to the right and are now about eight miles from the city of Savannah. As you have heard when this reaches you the 2nd Division of our Corps under General Hazen charged and took Fort McAllister at the head of Ossibow Sound and at the mouth of the Ogeechee River opening our communications with the rest of the world by way of the sea. This was done Tuesday Dec. 13.

On the fifteenth of December, General Howard's headquarters were at Anderson's Plantation, about eight miles from Savannah. Howard's wing extended from the canal to along the Little Ogeechee River to the extreme right. By the sixteenth, steamboats had been able to get as far as King's Bridge, bringing to the troops mail which had accumulated since the army had left Atlanta.

By the eighteenth of December, Savannah was still in a state of siege. General Hardee refused to surrender. Sherman decided to make more of an effort to surround Savannah on all sides, having three sides already cut off. Sherman then took a boat to Wassaw Sound and conferred with Admiral Dahlgren and General Foster on how pressure could be applied to General Hardee in Savannah. Upon his return, Sherman learned that Savannah had been evacuated by the morning of the twenty-first. Generals Howard and Slocum moved their headquarters into the city, and Sherman did likewise on December 22. On the same day, Sherman set a telegram to President Lincoln, to present him a Christmas gift of the city of Savannah.[35]

In a letter to General Sherman from General Grant, he said he told President Lincoln he would not have trusted Sherman's campaign to any other living commander.

In a letter to General Grant written December 24, Sherman said he didn't like to boast, but felt his army had the confidence that made it almost invincible. Also, when writing to General Halleck on the same day regarding the Fifteenth Corps, he said: "... if you have watched the history of that corps, you will have remarked that they generally do their work pretty well."[36]

Confederate General Hood, whom Sherman had been chasing in October, had made his way into Tennessee. On December 15 and 16, Hood had come up against General Thomas in Nashville, where he was soundly defeated. Hood then slipped southward over the Tennessee River and never again was an effective fighting force.

At this time, there were about 20,000 people living in Savannah. Major General John W. Geary, who commanded a division of the Twentieth Corps, had been the first to enter the city. He was selected to command the city, and acted as a kind of governor. Geary established a police force, which maintained order. Daily life of the citizens returned to a more normal state.

In Savannah, Georgia on December 27, 1864, Sam wrote to Mattie (Martha), his bride-to-be:

I very much regret to say that I cannot spend the Holy days with you; but since this is impossible I'm trying to spend them to the best advantage. As you have heard some days ago we entered Savannah on the evening of December 21st the enemy having evacuated the place that night previous. Since we entered the city I have been unusually busy making back returns. I have not yet quite completed the task; but tomorrow I think I can finish. Savannah as you know is a large city for the South. Business houses are all closed and consequently things go on very dull and one gets lonely. I think that before long houses will be opened. Our regiment is doing provost guard duty and we're having very good times. Duty is pretty severe, but we do not mind that as long as we have so comfortable a situation. The regiment is camped in a park and the officers are quartered in a four-story brick close by. We have everything necessary convenient. Provisions here have been a little scarce,

The March to The Sea

but a good and abundant supply is being landed today. We have a daily newspaper published in the city. I mailed the first copy to you a few days ago. I sent it simply because it was the first Union paper printed in Savannah since the breaking out of the rebellion. I suppose the paper will be continued I hope so for by it we can get later news than from the northern papers. Then to we can get the local news. I do not know whether it is intended we shall remain here during the winter or not. I cannot yet see any indications of a move. It may be that since we have been detached to do provost guard duty we may be left here when our Division moves. This, however, is altogether uncertain. The troops who garrison Savannah will have a "nice thing." I think it is no more than right that we should have a share of the nice things of the Army and here's the place I would like to have mine located. I have not heard from you or from home since the capture of Savannah and I am very anxiously looking for a letter if not several. I would like to hear if you have received those "views about Chattanooga" and how you like them. They are not as well executed as they might have been; yet they are quite natural. I suppose Chattanooga is considerably changed since I left it. We were constantly at work fortifying the place when I left. We have cheering news from Nashville, Hood's Tennessee Campaign ending just as we of the Army prophesied. We were too well acquainted with the ground over which he had to pass to think that he could be anything else than unsuccessful. The fair prospects of the Rebels are certainly fast waning. One thing is very noticeable the rebels are not so impudent and saucy as they used to be. The tone of the Southerners today in Savannah is milder far than that of the citizens of Nashville and Louisville and Memphis to one year ago. I see the mayor of the city has called a meeting of the citizens to make arrangements with the General commanding. The citizens are very civil and I cannot see but they treat soldiers as well as they are treated in the North when they are not just at home. The churches were nearly all full last Sunday the pulpits being filled by their old pastors. How it was at the other churches I do not know. But at the Presbyterian Church a large portion of the congregation was soldiers. The minister was very cautious not to say anything disrespectful of the government at Washington. In fact he studiously avoided saying anything concerning our national troubles although his subject—special provinces—would very naturally lead him to them. I do not know whether the present ministers will be allowed to remain. Whether they are or not I suppose will depend on how they conduct themselves and what stand they take of things in regard to questions of national interest. They will doubtless be careful not to cause a collision with the military authorities. General Sherman has been reviewing the troops composing this army for the last three days; day before yesterday the 15th Corps, yesterday the 17th, today the 14th and tomorrow I believe he is reviewing the 20th Corps. Some think this an indication of an early move. Whether it is or not time will decide. We cannot well move just now for we have not supplies for a campaign. Whether we go on a campaign or not we have about eight months to serve and so it makes a little difference to us whether the 15th Corps rests or not. I hope that by the time the war will end.

Chapter Six

The March Through the Carolinas

On January 2, 1865, Sherman was authorized to march northward with the army. The Seventeenth Corps was transferred by steamer to Beaufort Island, South Carolina. By the tenth, General Howard, who commanded the right wing of the army, had most of his Seventeenth Corps there. On the tenth, the right wing began their march for Pocotaligo, South Carolina, which was twenty-five miles inland. Arriving at Pocotaligo on the fifteenth, the Seventeenth Corps found the fort abandoned.[37]

General Slocum turned Savannah over to General J.G. Foster on January 18. Sherman made the first general order to move on the nineteenth. On the twenty-second of January, Sam wrote two short notes home, which showed he was near Beaufort, South Carolina.[38]

February 1, 1865 was the date designated for the army to begin its move northward. The composition of the army was basically the same as that which had marched from Atlanta to Savannah. Major General John A. Logan had returned and was in charge of the Fifteenth Army Corps. Brigadier General Charles R. Woods was in command of the First Division. Major General Oliver O. Howard was in command of the right wing, composed of the Fifteenth and Seventeenth Corps.[39] As the army moved, the right wing marched up the Salkiehatchie River. The Fifteenth Corps moved by Hickory Hill to Beaufort's Bridge. General Sherman traveled with the Fifteenth Corps through McPhersonville and Hickory Hill. On the third, the Fifteenth Corps arrived at Beaufort's Bridge. A rebel force occupied the opposite shore. Two brigades managed to get across the river and routed the Confederates, who promptly abandoned the defensive front along the Salkiehatchie. The Fifteenth Corps then crossed the river at Beaufort's Bridge. On February 6, the Fifteenth Corps was five miles from Bamberg. The following day, Sherman, with the Fifteenth Corps, reached the railroad. Soon the soldiers were tearing up and destroying track. As this was an important railroad, Sherman wanted to destroy it for fifty miles. By the ninth, the Fifteenth Corps was at Blackville. Two days later, the troops were ready to make their next move to Orangeburg. Confederate General Wheeler's cavalry had been hovering and skirmishing around the army from the beginning of the march. In fact, his presence had been felt since leaving Atlanta. Wheeler's whereabouts had to be considered when various movements were underway. On the move to Columbia, Union cavalry commander Kilpatrick was to protect the left flank from Wheeler when he was detected.[40]

The South Edisto River was crossed on the eleventh. The next day, the troops were bearing down on Orangeburg. Taking this town would break communications between Charleston and Columbia. The bridge over the Edisto River was gone, and some Confederate troops were present across the river. General Blair was sent downriver to make a crossing, which hastened the withdrawal of the rebels. The bridge was repaired and the troops crossed over.

The March Through the Carolinas

Sherman was with the Fifteenth Corps on the thirteenth of February as they crossed the North Edisto River at Snilling's Bridge. Now they turned toward Columbia. By evening, the Fifteenth Corps was twenty-one miles from Columbia. It was here that Sherman learned that Columbia had been all but abandoned by General Hardee, who had supposed Sherman was headed for Charleston. The next day, Charles R. Woods's division (Sam's) of the Fifteenth Corps reached the Little Congaree River about seven miles below Columbia. The leading brigade skirmished forward and discovered the bridge was gone. On the other side of the river was a fairly large number of Confederate soldiers. A brigade was sent to the left to find a way to cross the river. Soon the brigade crossed the Little Congaree and opened a way on the main road. Woods's skirmishers then crossed over and work began to repair the bridge, which was accomplished within an hour.

About a half mile from here, a foraging party was attacked by a group of rebel cavalry. The charge was met by General Woods's skirmish line, which drove the cavalry off.[41]

The Fifteenth Corps reached the Congaree River across from Columbia on February 16. They continued upstream for three miles and crossed over the river. Not far from the opposite side, they came to the Broad River and found the bridge in flames. Butler's cavalry had just crossed the bridge on the way to Columbia. During the night of the sixteenth, General Howard had moved Stone's brigade of Woods's division (Sam's) of the Fifteenth Corps across the river by rafts made from pontoons. The brigade then gave protection as a pontoon bridge was constructed. At about nine or ten in the morning, Colonel Stone met with the mayor of Columbia, who came out to surrender the city. Sherman instructed Stone to go to Columbia with the mayor, and the brigade would follow when the bridge was completed.[42]

General Sherman and his staff passed over the bridge, followed by General Howard and his staff. Then came General Logan, leading General Charles R. Woods and the rest of the Fifteenth Corps. The army marched up the hill, seeing old fields of corn and cotton. Upon entering the city, many people—white and black—filled the streets. A fire was burning near the market square. A high wind was causing it to spread. Here Stone's brigade had halted, stacked arms, and were busy with some citizens in trying to extinguish a fire in some rows of cotton bales. Sherman was told the fire had been started by Confederate cavalry as they left the city. Farther along, a part of Stone's brigade was separating good from bad corn and cornmeal, which had partially burned near a large storehouse that had burned to the ground.[43]

General Howard was put in charge of Columbia. The Fifteenth Corps marched through the city during the afternoon of the seventeenth, and proceeded to the Winnsboro and Camden roads. General Howard's troops were destroying railroad tracks on the eighteenth and nineteenth. Leaving Columbia in ruins on the twentieth, the Fifteenth Corps with the right wing marched northward toward Winnsboro. Winnsboro was reached on the twenty-first. From Winnsboro, the right wing went toward the east to Cheraw and then to Fayetteville, North Carolina. Heavy rains caused the Catawba River to rise, which made crossing it very difficult. When a pontoon bridge broke, the Fourteenth Corps was left on the west bank. It took several days to get the Fourteenth Corps across. On the twenty-seventh, the left wing continued on its march to Cheraw. The roads were very bad and needed to be corduroyed much of the way. The village of Chesterfield was reached on the second of March. Here General Sherman learned that Howard was already in Cheraw, South Carolina. General Hardee thought the Union Army was on its way to Charlotte, and had sent a great many supplies to Cheraw. These were now in Union hands. What could not be used was destroyed. The army had mostly crossed the Pedee River near Cheraw by March 6. On that date, the army marched for Fayetteville, the Fifteenth Corps taking a direct road. The Fifteenth Corps reached Laurel Hill, North Carolina on March 8, and on the

The March Through the Carolinas

ninth were near a small church called Bethel. Heavy rain forced to troops to corduroy the roads, on which it had become very difficult to travel. Sherman arrived at Fayetteville on the eleventh. General Hardee and Wade Hampton with his cavalry had just escaped over the Cape Fear River. Hampton burned the bridge as he left town. The whole army was at Fayetteville on the eleventh, and preparations were made to construct two pontoon bridges.[44] March 12 was a Sunday, and the army rested as General Sherman said: "... from the toils and labors of six weeks of as hard marching has ever fell to a lot of soldiers."[45]

In writing to General Grant on March 12, Sherman described the army: "The Army is in splendid health, condition, and spirits, though we have had foul weather, and roads that would have stopped travel to almost any other body of men I have ever heard of."[46]

Sherman crossed the Cape Fear River on the thirteenth and fourteenth. The next day, the army marched for Goldsboro. Both wings were instructed to hold four divisions, each in readiness for instant battle. The left wing was met with stubborn resistance on the fifteenth and sixteenth by General Hardee's infantry, artillery, and cavalry. On the sixteenth, a general battle broke out near Averysboro. The Confederates were defeated after their line was caught in flank. The next day, Hardee was in full retreat.[47]

On the eighteenth, the left wing was marching toward Goldsboro, and by evening was about five miles from Bentonsville. Near Bentonsville, the left wing encountered Johnston's army, and a battle ensued. Sherman had just left Slocum's left wing to join Howard's right wing when he learned of the battle. Immediately, the Fifteenth Corps was turned toward Bentonsville. By early morning of the next day, the Fifteenth Corps with General Charles R. Woods's division leading approached Bentonsville. The Fifteenth Corps lined up with General Slocum's forces during the day and were joined by two divisions of the Seventeenth Corps. Sherman decided to be defensive, as he was expecting General Schofield and General Terry to be in Goldsboro on the twenty-first. About noon on the twenty-first, General Mower of the First Division of the Seventeenth Corps attacked and broke through the rebel line. This not being part of Sherman's plan, Mower was ordered back to his lines. Sherman later came to regret his decision. The next day (the twenty-second), Johnston's army had retreated to Smithfield. On the twenty-second, the march resumed, and during the twenty-third and twenty-fourth, the whole army was at Goldsboro, having been joined by General Terry with two divisions of the Tenth Corps and General Schofield with the Twenty-third Corps.[48]

General Sherman sums up the march in this way:

> Thus was concluded one of the longest and most important marches ever made by an organized army in a civilized country. The distance from Savannah to Goldsboro is four hundred twenty-five miles, and the route traversed embraced five large navigable rivers, viz., the Edisto, Broad, Catawba, Pedee and Cape Fear, at either of which a comparatively small force, well handled, should have made the passage most difficult, if not impossible. The country generally was in a state of nature, with innumerable swamps, with simply mud roads, nearly every mile of which had to be corduroyed. In our route we had captured Columbia, Cheraw, and Fayetteville, important cities and depots of supplies, had compelled the evacuation of Charleston City and Harbor, and utterly broken up all the railroads of South Carolina, and had consumed a vast amount of food and forage, essential to the enemy for the support of his own armies. We had in mid-winter accomplished the whole journey of four hundred and twenty-five miles in fifty days, averaging ten miles per day, allowing ten lay-days, and had reached Goldsboro with the army in superb order, and the trains almost as fresh as when we had started from Atlanta.[49]

The March Through the Carolinas

At Goldsboro the last of March, Sherman took some time to rest and re-outfit his army. New units were added to the army, which was then reorganized. The reorganized army was divided into three groups: the Army of the Tennessee, Major General O. O. Howard commanding; the Army of Georgia, Major General H. W. Slocum commanding; and the Army of the Ohio, Major General John M. Schofield commanding. These were the right wing, the left wing, and the center, respectively. The Fifteenth Corps was still commanded by Major General John A. Logan. The First Division was commanded by Brevet Major General C. R. Woods, and the Third Brigade (Sam's) was commanded by Colonel G. A. Stone. During this time, March 27 and 28, Sherman traveled to City Point on the James River, where he met with General Grant and President Lincoln and others. Sherman remarked of Lincoln: "Of all the men I ever met, he seemed to possess more of the elements of greatness combined with goodness, than any other."[50]

General Sherman was back in Goldsboro on March 30. After devising a plan of action detailed in "Special Field Orders, No 48" Sherman learned on April 6 that Richmond and Petersburg had fallen. Lee's army and Confederate government officials had fled the Richmond area toward Danville. Sherman quickly altered his plans, and on April 10 moved the army toward Smithfield, where Joe Johnston's army was. Smithfield was reached on the eleventh, and the Confederate army was found to have retreated toward Raleigh, burning the bridges as they moved. The remainder of the day was spent repairing the bridges. That night, Sherman received word that General Lee had surrendered to General Grant at Appomattox, Virginia on April 9.[51] General Sherman's announcement to his army, dated April 12, 1865, is as follows:

> The general commanding announces to the army that he has official notice from General Grant that General Lee surrendered to him his entire army, on the ninth inst., at Appomattox Court-House, Virginia.

Glory to God and our country, and all honor to our comrades in arms, toward whom we are marching!

A little more labor, a little more toil on our part, the great race is won, and our Government stands regenerated, after four long years of war.

W. T. Sherman, Major General Commanding[52]

THE SURRENDER OF JOSEPH JOHNSTON

The question of Joe Johnston then remained. Sherman pushed into Raleigh, North Carolina on April 13. He then directed his forces toward Asheville. Other Union cavalry units were also bearing down in this area. General Stoneman's cavalry from East Tennessee was near Salisbury. General Sheridan's cavalry was headed for Raleigh from Appomattox. Elsewhere, General Wilson's cavalry had moved through parts of Alabama into Georgia, near Macon.[53]

On the fourteenth, Sherman received a letter from General Johnston, proposing surrender. A meeting between generals Sherman and Johnston was set for the seventeenth, midway between Durham and Hillsboro. Sherman had entered a train car, awaiting departure, when he received an urgent message that announced the assassination of President Lincoln. Keeping the message secret, Sherman continued by train to Durham, then by horse about five miles, where he met Johnston. It was decided to use a Mr. Bennett's house to negotiate the surrender. At the beginning of the meeting, Sherman revealed to Johnston Lincoln's assassination, which caused Johnston considerable consternation. The meeting continued, and agreement was reached to meet the next day to make final arrangements. The next day, the generals again met. General Sherman wrote out the terms of surrender, and the document was signed. The terms of surrender were then sent to Washington D.C. for certification.[54] The morning of the twenty-fourth of April, General Grant arrived by train to Raleigh. Grant brought with him the message that Sherman's surrender terms were not accepted. Sherman immediately sent a message to Johnston, informing him of the situation. Sherman then demanded surrender on the same terms as those given at Appomattox. On April 26, the generals again met at the Bennetts' house. The new agreement was promptly signed.[55]

Chapter Seven

The Grand Review

General Sherman called his corps commanders together on April 28, and reviewed with them the plans for the future. The first step involved the left and right wings, who were to march north with their generals to Richmond, Virginia. On May 7, Sherman arrived in Richmond and found his army encamped in and around Manchester. Sherman received orders on May 10 to continue the march to Alexandria, Virginia, which is just across the Potomac River from Washington D.C. The army began its march on May 11, passing through Richmond. The right wing, under General Logan, started their march on the twelfth. General John A. Logan was now in command of the right wing and the army of the Tennessee. General Howard had been called to Washington to run the new Bureau of Refugees, Freedmen, and Abandoned Lands. The right wing, as it marched, went by Fredericksburg. During the nineteenth and twentieth of May, the whole army had reached Alexandria and made camp. On the nineteenth, Sherman received a copy of an order that called for a grand review. The order came from the president and the Cabinet, and would include the armies who were near Washington. General Meade's army would march on the twenty-third, and General Sherman's army would march on the twenty-fourth.[56]

Captain Samuel B. Heizer's last letter of the war was written from Camp Thirtieth Iowa Infantry Alexandria, Virginia May 21, 1865. He wrote as follows:

My Dear Brother

After a hard march of about 30 miles we got into "permanent camp" in plain view of and but a short distance from the city of Alexandria today. We can see the dome of the Capitol of United States have (and) a part of the city of Washington. Next Tuesday begins the greatest review (I suppose) that ever has or ever will take place in this country. I dread it. I dread any review but this one I must face. We (i.e.) Sherman's army as you have already learned are to be reviewed on Wednesday the 24th. I hope I may be able to find some excuse for not being on duty that day so that I may escape it. On our way from Richmond we passed Mount Vernon, the residence and burial place of General Washington. I was well-paid for the march of about five miles out of the way although we didn't get to stop, only march through the grounds and tomb at a slow time and then pass on. I would like to see it again when I could have more time to see what is to be seen.

This is Sunday evening, it has been raining almost all day but has ceased now. I have not been very well today. I have a slight attack of diarrhea. I am, however, on duty as officer of the day. The boys are well. Mark and Dave Carmean are very well. All are anxious to be mustered out and paid off and sent home. There is some talk of sending us to Iowa to be paid off. This the soldiers think unfair. It is virtually saying a soldier is incapable of controlling himself. I will keep your money in order that you may not spend it until you get nearer home. This would be very ungrateful in our authorities.

The Grand Review

If anyone in the world has a right to use his money it is the patriot soldier. Then too many Western soldiers as not wish to go must. Some want to buy government horses or mules to take home with them for farming. But I must stop.

Very Truly Yours
Sam B. Heizer

General Sherman was on the reviewing stand on the twenty-third as General Meade's army marched by. He said, "Today was beautiful, and the pageant was superb."[57] During the afternoon and evening of the twenty-third, Sherman's army crossed Long Bridge and encamped in the streets around the Capitol.

In the following passage, General Sherman ably and skillfully described the Grand Review of the twenty-fourth of May, 1865:

This morning of the 24th was extremely beautiful, and the ground was in splendid order for our review. The streets were filled with people to see the pageant, armed with bouquets of flowers for their favorite regiments or heroes, and everything was propitious. Punctually at 9 am the signal-gun was fired, when in person, attended by General Howard and all my staff, I rode slowly down Pennsylvania Avenue, the crowds of men, women, and children, densely lining the sidewalks, and almost obstructing the way. We were followed close by General Logan and the head of the 15th Corps. When I reached the Treasury-building, and looked back, the site was simply magnificent. The column was compact, and the glittering muskets looked like a solid mass of steel, moving with the regularity of a pendulum. We passed the Treasury-building, in front of which and of the White House was an immense throng of people, for whom extensive stands had been prepared on both sides of the avenue. As I neared the brick house opposite the lower corner of Lafayette Square, someone asked me to notice Mr. Seward, who, still feeble and bandaged for his wounds, had been removed there that he might behold the troops. I moved in that direction and took off my hat to Mr. Seward, who sat at an upper window. He recognized the salute, returned it, and then we rode on steadily past the President, saluting with our swords. All on his stand arose and acknowledged the salute. Then, turning into the gate of the presidential grounds, we left our horses with orderlies, and went upon the stand, where I found Mrs. Sherman, with her father and son. Passing them, I shook hands with the President, General Grant, and each member of the cabinet. As I approached Mr. Stanton, he offered me his hand, but I declined it publicly, and the fact was universally noticed. I then took my post on the left of the President, and for six hours and a half stood, while the army passed in the order of the Fifteenth, Seventeenth, and Fourteenth Corps. It was, in my judgment, the most magnificent army in existence—sixty-five thousand men in splendid physique, who had just completed a march of nearly two thousand miles in hostile country, in good drill, and who realized that they were being completely scrutinized by thousands of their fellow-countrymen and by foreigners. Division after division passed, each commander of an army corps or division coming on the stand during the passage of his command, to be presented to the President, cabinet, and spectators. The steadiness and firmness of the tread, the careful dress on the guides, the uniform intervals between the companies, all eyes directly to the front, and the tattered and bullet-riven flags, festooned with flowers, all attracted universal notice. Many good people, up to that time, had looked upon our Western army as a sort of mob; but the world then saw, and recognized the fact, that it was an army in the proper sense, well-

The Grand Review

organized, well commanded and disciplined; and there was no wonder that it had swept through the South like a tornado. For six hours and a half that strong trend of the Army of the West resounded along Pennsylvania Avenue; not a soul of that vast crowd of spectators left his place; and, when the rear of the column had passed by, thousands of spectators still lingered to express their sense of confidence in the strength of a Government which could claim such an army.... On the whole, the grand review was a splendid success, and was a fitting conclusion to the campaign and the war.[58]

Major General William T. Sherman summed up his war experiences in his general orders when he took leave from the army:

[Special Field Orders, No. 76]

Headquarters Military Division of the Mississippi, in the Field, Washington, D.C., May 30, 1865

The general commanding announces to the Army of the Tennessee and Georgia that the time has come for us to part. Our work is done, and armed enemies no longer defy us. Some of you will go to your homes, and others will be retained in military service till further orders. And now that we are about to separate, to mingle with the civil world, it becomes a pleasing duty to recall to mind the situation of natural affairs when, but little more than a year ago, we were gathered about the cliffs of Lookout Mountain, and all the future was wrapped in doubt and uncertainty. Three armies had come together from distant fields, with separate histories, yet bound to one common cause—the union of our country, and the perpetuation of our inheritance. There is no need to recall to your memories Tunnel Hill, with Rocky-Face Mountain and Buzzard-Roost Gap, and the ugly forts of Dalton behind. We were in earnest, and paused not for danger and difficulty, but dashed through Snake-Creek Gap and fell on Resaca; then on to the Etowah, to Dallas, Kennesaw; and the heats of summer found us on the banks of the Chattahoochee, far from home, and dependent on a single road for supplies. Again we were not to be held by any obstacle, and crossed over and fought four hard battles for the possession of the citadel of Atlanta. That was the crisis of our history. A doubt still clouded our future, but we solved the problem, destroyed Atlanta, struck boldly across the State of Georgia, severed all the main arteries of life to our enemy, and Christmas found us at Savannah. Waiting there only long enough to fill our wagons, we again began a march which, for peril, labor, and results, will compare with any other ever made by an organized army. The floods of the Savannah, the swamps of the Combahee and Edisto, the "high hills" and rocks of the Santee, the flat quagmires of the Pedee and Cape Fear Rivers, were all passed in mid-winter, with its floods and rains, in the face of and accumulating enemy; and, after the battles of Averysboro and Bentonsville, we once more came out of the wilderness, to meet our friends at Goldsboro. Even then we paused only long enough to get new clothing, to reload our wagons, again pushed on to Raleigh and beyond, until we met our enemy suing for peace, instead of war, and offering to submit to the injured laws of his and our country. As long as the enemy was defiant, nor mountains nor rivers, nor swamps, nor hunger, nor cold, had checked us; but when he, who had fought us hard and persistently, offered submission, your general thought it wrong to pursue him farther, and negotiations followed, which resulted, as you all know, in his surrender. How far the operations of this army contributed to the final overthrow of the Confederacy and the peace which now dawns upon us, must be judged by others, not by us; but that you have

The Grand Review

done all that men could do has been admitted by those in authority, and we have a right to join in the universal joy that fills our land because the war is over, and our Government stands vindicated before the world by the joint action of the volunteer armies and navy of the United States. To such as remain in the service, your general need only remind you that success in the past was due to hard work and discipline, and that the same work and discipline are equally important in the future. To such as go home, he will only say that our favored country is so grand, so extensive, so diversified in climate, soil, and productions, that every man may find a home and occupation suited to his taste; none should yield to the natural impatience sure to result from our past life of excitement and adventure. You will be invited to seek new adventures abroad; do not yield to the temptation, for it will lead only to death and disappointment. Your general now bids you farewell, with the full belief that, as in war you have been good soldiers, so in peace you'll make good citizens; and if, unfortunately, new war should arise in our country, "Sherman's army" will be the first to buckle on its old armor, and come forth to defend and maintain the Government of our inheritance.

By order of Major General W. T. Sherman
L. M. Dayton, Assistant Adjutant General.[59]

Part Two

The Civil War Letters of Samuel B. Heizer

Letter 1

June 24, 1862

My Dear Father,

    I write to you in great haste this morning. I shall start home Thursday afternoon and will get to Burlington Saturday evening, probably not before 4:00 and maybe later. If you can conveniently be in town or send someone it will save some expense. If you cannot if it be not too late to I will try and walk home. I don't know whether my foot will be able to bear the walk or not.
        All is well.
        Yours, S B Heizer

Letter 2

Camp Iowa Company "C"
Keokuk, Iowa
August 31, 1862

My Dear Mother,

    Yours of the 27th was received a day or two ago, and I have been so busy that I have not had time to write until now and now as I have time I must gladly perform a task which I would willingly do every day if I had time and opportunity.

    You know I have often spoken of the orderly's duties and I find them fully as laborious as I expected. But I think it much better for me to be busy all the time than if it were otherwise. You will know the influence of idleness envoys. So you needn't be troubled about my work. As you have already heard our quarters are excellent our rations are good as we could reasonably ask and the boys as far as I can judge from appearances in very good spirits. I hear that someone told at your suit that our company was in a state of mutiny. Now I want you to understand that the man who said that told a base falsehood. Some of the boys expressed some dissatisfaction at the delay in mustering us into U. S. service. But that we were in a state of mutiny is unqualifiedly false and the man who said so should receive the hisses of Des Moines (?). Then in regard to the poisoning you mentioned there are some reasons for thinking that the boys were poisoned although (those?) being sick may have been the result of eating too much trash. At first-off they had been poisoned but have come to the conclusion that they (?) Gorged with pies, cakes and other such things and the poison had nothing to do with it. Now this is only my opinion and you'll have to take it for what it is worth. There has been talk ever since we arrived that we would be paid in a day or two. If we are paid in a week from today I shall be perfectly satisfied and a little surprised. We will probably be paid in two days after the regiment which is the 30th is full. There are at present but seven companies mustered. The other three are yet to come. The report was in camp that we would go to Mt. Pleasant. But that is a ridiculous idea has long as there are not men enough here to fill the 30th and when the 36th is yet to be filled and quartered here. Some of the fresh fans believe a great many such reports but you can't fool our Iowa first in any such way. I think we will be company "C" of the 30th regiment just as good a position as we had asked. Company " C" would please Capt. Roberts, because then he would be senior captain and in the absence of the field officer would command the regiment. For the men however it will be better and less (?). So I would be glad to get to company " C". I would like to see you and father and all folks in camp. I know you would be pleased with our position as I am. Some of the boys took blankets, as we have not received any yet. At first the boys would have straw in their bunks but in our (?) It is all out to and they think pine boards a soft bed. If I had time I would fill another sheet and not tell all but as it is I must close.

  Your affectionate son,
  Sam

Letter 3

Helena, Arkansas
Monday Morning, December 8th 1862

My Dear Parents

Having returned from an expedition into Mississippi and having had a nights rest I now propose to give you a brief account of our doings first giving you the no doubt pleasing news that during the whole time of our absence Luther and I were very well and able to march with the company. In fact, such a trip will ensure good health to any command. But for the history of the expedition one week ago last Thursday, 11 days ago this very morning we left our camp at Helena. Thirty-five men having been detailed from our company including no commissioned privates, and our company. Bugler Robs - McMillian - Lieut. Creighton were the only commissioned with our company the order for this detail from the company (?) who would command us. The entire force sent was estimated by those who have an opportunity of knowing, had 8000 strong. At 1 o'clock the whole force had been put aboard the boats and immediately turned southward and landed on the Mississippi side at a place called Delta. It took the greater part of the night to unload the boats. Early the next morning we were started on the road leading a little south of east. I should have said that the whole force was under the command of Brigadier General Hovey, Generals Washburn and Wyman having commands subordinate to Hovey. The first days march was a hard one for new troops who had never before marched over five miles at a time and that through the streets of St. Louis to Benton Barracks. We halted a few minutes about noon and ate a little then marched till evening making the entire days march about 25 miles. It was dark when we camped or rather stopped for the night (for we had no tents and very little else with us except our knapsacks and blankets). The boys were very tired and as soon as they could get a little supper most of them lay down to rest and sleep which they very much needed. Luther and I however sat up till midnight if not later cooking (?) For our meals for the next day which Birdwell had skirmished on the road a mile and a half back of our camping ground. It was as good meat as ever I ate. It was very fat and very tender. During the evening, soon after the boys had begun to lay down Dr. Walker one of our surgeons, the only one with us, came round with a bucket of as good whiskey as is manufactured giving each one of the regiment a glass for which he received the thanks of all concerned. No difference how good temperance man (?) and everyone took his drink with a good will only wishing he could have twice as much. I never before saw an instance where I thought a well man benefited by the use of ardent spirits. I suppose some of our good brothers think this all wrong. But let them be placed in the same situation and they would do likewise. However, I will not discuss the subject now. When we had finished frying beef we lay down on a soldier's couch under the open heavens for a nights repose and sweet dreams of the dear ones at home. Saturday morning at an early hour we were waked from our slumber by the bugle, our breakfast was hastily dispatched and we put upon the road. This morning we were told to keep our places as nearly as possible so that if we were attacked we could fall in line of battle in the minutes warning. We moved on however without any disturbance from the enemy, arriving at the Tallahatchee River at the mouth of the Coldwater in the evening only stopping on the way to eat a few bites of hard cracker and water at (?). After we had our supper and drawn rations we were called into line and marched over the river, a pontoon bridge having been placed over the stream during the day. We immediately went into camp on the other side of the river tearing down a stable and carrying rails from the nearest fence for our fires. We all expected to be called up early next morning and put on the march. But whether it was Sunday or for some other reason we did not march that day I cannot tell. I suppose however it was for some other reason. For I have seen nothing so far to prove to me that General Hovey cares anymore for Sunday than any other day. During the forenoon Lt. Col. Torrance who was the only Field Officer with the regiment called us into line forming nearly a circle around him. He then made some very appropriate remarks about our situation read from one of the Psalms and commented upon it. He advised all to read the Bible. Said he loved the Book. Thanked God that he had been raised by parents who had taught him to read it. Lieut. Ford of Company F then made a short prayer when we were dismissed. Let me say the more we have to do with Lt. Col. Torrance the more we love him. The regiment almost idolizes him while they despise Col. Abbott and Major Denicy. During the evening there was preaching in camp by Lt. Ford (the chaplain was not allowed to go with us, because the greater part of the regiment was left at Helena). I with several others of our company went to preaching at the 28th Iowa who are next to us. Our Company will not hear Lieut. Ford because he is a Democrat. Nine-tenths of our company would as soon listen to a Southern secessionist as a northern Democrat. As for myself I would rather. I despise a Democrat more than I do a traitor. Just as I used to say a northern Democrat sympathizer is worst than a Southern traitor. I believe in burning and destroying all kinds of property we cannot use ourselves or hinder the rebels from using in any way. After we had lain down that night a storm of rain came up which soaked our blankets completely while it had but little effect upon us. Our blankets soak up so much water that it has to rain a long time to soak us. Our clothes were a little damp in the morning but not enough to amount to much. We succeeded during the day Monday in drying ourselves and blankets pretty well. Some however had pretty heavy blankets when evening came. At 4:00 in the evening the bugle sounded for the command to fall in. Cannonading had been heard in front and it was supposed a battle was coming on. We were therefore hurried on about six miles when a messenger came back giving the news that it was but a skirmish of cavalry and flying artillery. We therefore were ordered to camp in a pasture field nearby. Tuesday morning we were pushed on and in the evening came to the bluff, crossed over one hill and camped in a hollow. It rained on us this day and we did not march as far as usual. We had then marched nearly 60 miles from the Mississippi and all over bottomland. Such a bottom I never expected to see. I had no idea that anyplace was the Mississippi bottom 60 miles wide. The greater part of this land is in time of high water either overflowed or surrounded with water. We could see on the trees a mark of high water by the difference of color of the lower mark. It was colored yellow. In this bottom are large cypress swamps around which there are immense cypress forests. Many of the trees I should think were 150 feet high and so close together that one can see but a short distance, this fact taken with two others that there are no limbs for near 75 feet and that there is no undergrowth would very naturally make one think the trees pretty thickly set in the ground. There is no prairie land that we could discover in all this space. I suppose there is none for hundreds of miles on either side of the road we traveled. If you want a wooded farm come here. The plantations are generally pretty large but not cultivated just as well as they might be. I suppose the want of proper cultivation is due to the rebellious government of Jeff Davis pressing men into the Army and to the fact that the slaves have not worked when there is no overseer. There are but very few good buildings. I expected to see on these plantations splendid mansions. But not so. I saw one pretty well arranged place. It seemed as if the planter might have been a pretty good manager. In one of his fields was a large flock of sheep I suppose 300. I failed to say in the proper place that at the Tallahatchee where we crossed on the bridge the Cavalry brought in several prisoners. But to continue the story Wednesday morning we pushed on. This morning we left all the forces except two canon of the first Iowa battery, 1800 cavalry and the detachments of the 28th and 30th Iowa infantry about 700 from the two. The cavalry pushed ahead the battery followed and we with the 28th Iowa marched along as fast as we could. And noon we halted beside a small stream for water and to eat a luncheon crackers and water of course. Soon after dinner if dinner it could be called Col. Torrance called us into line and said they were fighting (to use his own expression) like the devil in front and that we were ordered to come up on double quick. We did not exactly double quick; but we went as fast as we could sometimes running till we found the enemy had retreated. We however continued to advance till we came to a small town and railroad station called "Oakland" where we camped. The Col. assigned a large stone house two stories high and two smaller houses to our regiment. I say a large stone house, I mean a large one for the size of the town. Most of us preferred the open heavens to a building and made our beds outside where our guns were stacked. But first hogs were killed and cooked and eaten. A large amount of sweet potatoes, cornmeal, sugar, salt (which is a rarity in Dixie) and other things were divided among the companies of the two regiments. We had boiled pork roasted and boiled sweet potatoes, mushy turnips for supper. Besides this the boys got persimmons a few (?) from (?) which we kept eating till we could eat no more. That was a jolly night for the 30th. I found the paper upon which this letter is written in the storehouse assigned to our regiment. The next morning I was pretty sick for a while. I had made a hog of myself and of course must suffer the consequences. Persimmons enough for a company were still scattered on the ground. Had we known how much we were exposed that night we would not have been so jolly nor would we have slept soundly. The cavalry here brought in several men who had come to them and given themselves up. They had been forced into the rebel ranks and at this their first opportunity they had come to the federal lines. Now I only give this for what it's worth. I saw the prisoners brought in but what they said or how they happened to be taken I cannot swear to. I give it as I heard it. This morning just one week from the time we left Helena we turned back to travel again the road we had been traveling. You may think from what I have said that the expedition effected but little. You must remember, though, that I have related but little except what I saw. The cavalry burned two bridges of the railroad 40 miles apart which completely cut off Price's retreat (?) as also it did the means of reinforcing him by this (?) his supplies. Grant can now fight him and he (?) or let his own legs carry him to Vicksburg. Our retreat was hurried. We had ventured within a few miles of a large army with about 8000 men and struck a blow which he cannot very well recover from soon. Nothing of much consequence occurred during the retreat except hard marching. One man of the 28th Iowa was shot by a guerrilla within fifteen rods of his regiment the last night before we reached Helena. It is reported that the guerrilla was afterward shot by our men. This I cannot vouch for. The man shot was brought back to camp and buried today. We reached camp yesterday at noon. But our man in that part of the regiment that was away was brought back sick. Our regiment and the 28th especially ours has received the highest praise for our courage, our orderly conduct, our discipline and in cheerful endurance of hardship.

But I have time to write no more at present.

    As ever
    Your Affectionate Son
    Sam B. Heizer

Letter 4

In Camp Opposite Vicksburg
March 2nd 1863

My Dear Parents,

It is a beautiful Sunday morning and I have seated myself outside of the tent to write what should have been written a week ago if I had had the opportunity. Your letter together with the stamps and "Greenbacks" reached me just about a week ago. I was not expecting any money; but as it was it was very acceptable. The stamps came just in time for I was entirely out. Some of the boys that I had borrowed money of some time ago amounting to about 3 dollars were pleased when I presented to pay. I still have money enough when debt was paid to buy what little things I needed of which the paper that this is written on is one. I received Joseph's letter yesterday and he may expect an answer from me in a few days. Luther also received Edgar Blair's by the same mail. Joe must write oftener. He does well and if he were to write a while he would be able to write a long letter. Whether this is true or not, I do not know. I am, however, inclined to think that it is so, inasmuch as there is already due us six months pay. The rumor is that we will receive four months wages. If we do I will have $60 to send home. Our sick boys are doing pretty well. In the regiment, however, they are not so well. As high as three have died in our regimental hospital in one day. I am entirely well of my fever. My diarrhea is about cured which has been troubling me in my left leg is a great deal better. I have a terrible appetite and my only fears now are that I shall injure myself eating. Doctor tells me I must be very careful what I eat. Dave Carmean had a pretty hard time with rheumatism; but it is now a great deal better. He is walking about camp this morning. He did not have it as badly as he had at home. We have less than 20 privates for duty in our company now. I guess the talk about sending our regiment North was only talk. We were made to believe that every general that had anything to say in the matter had agreed to send us except Grant and that he had not been visited. Also that the Medical Director and Brigade Surgeon had signed the paper sending us North to remit our healths. This may all have been true enough but I doubt it. For I see no signs of a move. A report came to camp yesterday that a boat bearing a flag of truce had landed near us from the rebels and some of the boys thought they saw a white flag floating on the courthouse over the river, but my eyes could not see it. I think they were badly fooled and told them so. It almost made some of them angry when they felt sure they saw it with their own eyes. There is no doubt that two of our best boats are captured, the Steam Ram "Queen of the West "and the gunboat "Indianola ". So much for the strategical movement of running the blockade. The rebels I have no doubt expected such movement and prepared for it. From a parole prisoner belonging to the 26th Iowa from up the Arkansas River we have the report that Arkansas Post is again strongly fortified. If this be true we may have another brush there. Proctor was down to the mouth of the canal below the town and he says our men are building a strong fort there. How many guns it was to contain I do not remember; but its strength must be great. The canal is being enlarged as I suppose the newspapers have already informed you and now I have some confidence in the concern. Oh and must tell you a little circumstance that occurred last week. Our regiment was then all on picket duty below the canal. One evening we saw something coming down the river near our position. It looked very much like a gunboat and some thought it really was a gunboat. We soon found that it was only a wooden concern made just like a gunboat to deceive the rebels. The Rams which the rebels captured from us which were lying a few miles below skedaddled as soon as they saw this thing coming. We found on close observation that the boat was constructed entirely of wood and logs placed in the portals for guns. It did us great service in as much as there were no cannon with us and while the Rams were down the river a battery of guns were planted to defend the place and protect the men that were working on the canal. Had this not been done the rebels might have shelled us out and done mischief on the canal. They were so badly deceived that they continued to fire at her until she was out of range of their guns.

    But I must stop.
        I am as ever,
            Your Son Sam

Letter 5

Millikens Bend, Louisiana
April 30, 1863

My Dear Father and Mother,

You'll understand why have not written home for sometime back when I tell you that I have had a very sore boil on the back my right hand. It hurts me some to write but I can make out to scribble a little.

As you can see from the dating of this we have moved our camp since I last wrote. Day before yesterday we packed up in the morning and in the evening marched on the good steamer Edward Walsh. Soon after we found ourselves swiftly gliding up the broad Mississippi. It was a beautiful night clear except a small cloud in the north where occasionally lightning could be seen. At first our company was placed on the lower deck but that being very filthy, the boat not having been washed since a load of cattle had been on it, Capt. Roberts got permission to move us to the hurricane deck where we laid down and were soon in the land of dreams. Sometime during the night we landed at our present landing for we found ourselves tied up here in the morning. We enjoyed a good night's rest. During the forenoon we moved out from the river near a half-mile during the remainder of the day pitched our tents, policed the grounds and fitted up things generally. We have a good camping ground; good water within a half-mile and wood not very inconvenient. Altogether our move was quite a pleasant one and the change of position as far as convenience is concerned not useless. As far as military advantage is concerned I am altogether ignorant. I do not know the exact distance to Vicksburg: but think it about 30 miles.

A few days before we left our old camp the paymaster made his appearance and troubled us with two months wages. As the paymaster (Major Stanton) was going to Keokuk and he consented to do it; we sent our money home by him. He takes it to Keokuk and there expresses it to W. W. Harper in Burlington. You can get it by calling on him. The amount I sent is $35. He even told me I would not received any more for four months and I thought I would need the other five dollars before next payday. I had a little besides so that I have not need. Today we are mustered by General Thayer. It did us good to see his honest face. You need have no fears but that the 30th will follow wherever he leads. It is surprising how soon and how completely he has gained our confidence. There is no display about him. His hat is nothing but a common one without a feather. I believe I never saw him with the sash on. His clothes are very plain. He is a man of about 40, black hair and whiskers and pleasant countenance. He is of medium height and heavyset. More than that he is an admirer of "Iowa Boys" and will have no other in his brigade. But I must bid you good-bye. Luther and I are both quite well. You need not be scared if I do not write soon again for I think another boil is coming on my hand.

Tell Irene as soon as she writes to me I will write as good a letter as I can in return. I am looking for a letter from Joe.

Your Son Sam

Letter 6

Near Vicksburg, Mississippi
May 24th 1863

My Dear Parents,

You will no doubt hear of the dreadful but unsuccessful charges on our enemies works at this place day before yesterday, in which our regiment was engaged and in which we lost our Colonel and Major and 10 others and had 16 and wounded several of whom will doubtless die and one missing, before you receive this. Our Company suffered more than any other in the regiment. Losing out of 26 that went into the charge three killed and 13 wounded. All together since we came here our loss has been three killed and 14 wounded. Besides these our Captain and five men were knocked down by the explosion of shells but are now running about and not reported wounded. Our dead are Sergeant S.S.Perry and John E.Shapp and Patrick Ward. The wounded are R.P. Wycoff, Cyrus Hedges, T.U. Husted, W.H. Barnhill, T.F. Davis, J.T. Earnest, D.W. Hixon, R.B. Hixon, Wm U. Vaugh, Joseph Loyd, J.G. Bayles, G.H.Hully, and Wm Stewart. All these were wounded and the three killed in a few minutes. T. Speed Smith was slightly wounded Monday evening.

We have now present all told sick and well 31 men. Last night our regiment together with the rest of our brigade were moved back from the enemy's works some distance. When we stacked arms when we halted we had but ten well men to stack arms. It seemed as if Company C. was all gone. The place of the charge could not have been much worse for a charge if the rebels had made it being a high bluff and very steep with a short slope near the top not so steep. On the slow the men were butchered. General Thayer cried like a child when he saw the slaughter. I understand he was opposed to the charge in the first place. Some other regiments suffered about as bad as ours. Captain Roberts now commands the regiment Lt. Col. Torrance being at Milliken's Bend. I escaped without a scratch. Luther was well at Milliken's Bend when I left. I read a letter from David today and one from Mother. Mother's was dated the 10th of May. Dave's the 10th. I wrote from Perkins farm, Aclow, Carthage, and again from Jackson, Mississippi. But you may not have received the letters.

But I must stop.
    As Ever
    Your Son Sam
    P.S. I have no stamps.
    Would you send me a dollars worth. Sam

Letter 7

Black River Bridge
Mississippi August 20th 1863

My Dear Parents,
    I received your letter night before last and this afternoon as I am at leisure I shall attempt an answer. I commenced a letter last night; but being tired, sleepy, and lonesome, being alone I went to bed without finishing it and as I never like to write two or three times on the same sheet I shall spoil another. I have been very well since I wrote you last being troubled only with my finger. It is about well now and will be very tender for a good while. On that account I'm excused from Dress Parade but no other duty. I cannot handle the sword well enough while my finger continues sore to go out to Dress Parade. Our duty is quite light now and we have a splendid camp. We have, however, been quite unfortunate since Captain Creighton left us. Three of our men died within eight days from the time he left us. I told you of the two, Crawford and Henlly, when I wrote before. Since then just eight days from the time Captain left William Stewart died as we suppose from congestion of some kind as he seemed pretty well the day before he died. He told me at Dress Parade that he would not be able to go out with the company. I told him if he was sick he might stay in his quarters. Towards morning some of the men Gilson and Bell I believe heard someone groaning. At first they did not know what it meant. Pretty soon they heard it again. Bill got up and went over to Stewart's tent; for he was alone that night. Bell said to him Is that you Stuart what is the matter. He made no reply. He could still be heard breathing. Bill then went out to get a candle and light it and before he got back the life was gone from him. Gilson was some distance off and did not arrive till he was dead. The men did not wake me and I knew nothing of it till morning. There he passed away no one knowing what ailed him. But as there have been other cases of congestion of

bowels, lungs, and brain in these parts it was very naturally supposed to be one of these. The three men now lay side-by-side on a ridge just north of our camp. Four of these passed away suddenly an unexpectedly. All of them except one had been sick for a long time. We have four men in the company now that are very sick: but you're not acquainted with any of them. Dave Carmean is as well as I have ever known him and full of the mischief. There is no harm in his mischief. All of the Kossuth boys are as well as usual. Martin Luther is as busy as usual. It seems to me he never is still. He and Joe Pengh seem to make a complete team. It is now evening and I have a little time before roll call. The mail came in this evening but no letter for me. It was only a few stray letters that have been misclaimed. I look for letters every mail and when I do not get one from some source I am disappointed. If my friends are all as faithful as I try to be I would get letters oftener than I do. I get letters from home pretty regular however. I have no complaints to make of my own folks. I'm getting awful tired and guess I must stop. Besides I have about run out of news. I hope when Capt. Creighton gets back to camp to be able to make a short visit to Iowa. But I must stop.

    Yours truly
    Sam

P.S. A report came into camp today that orders have been given not to allow any more furloughs.
    How true it is I cannot say
    Yours Sam

Letter 8

Headquarters Co. C.
30th Iowa Infantry Volunteers
Black River, Mississippi
September 13th 1863

My Dear Parents

    I have been looking every mail for several weeks for a letter from home; but no letter comes. Our mail has been very light for a month or more. I believe I have not received a letter from home since Capt. Creighton left us.

    I suppose you are and have been busy and have not had much time for writing. I think though you might find time on Sunday. But I will not say much about it, for you may have good reason for not writing as I had not very long ago. Then it maybe some fault of the mailman; for several others of our company are in the same situation. I thought too that you might be waiting intending to send letters by Capt. Creighton. But none of these reasons can fill the place of a letter. We're living well now. We have cabbage in the head, canned tomatoes, new potatoes and occasionally milk, onions, fish, and green apples, besides our regular rations. So you can see that there's no danger of us starving yet a while at least.

    I had an attack of the intermittent fever about 10 days ago. But I have got bravely over that and am now enjoying as good health as I ever did. Quite a number of the company came down with the same complaint and some are not yet well although most of them are improving fast. Martin Luther was sick with it; but he is well again. We lost another man a few days ago by the name of Alvin H. Davis a young man from Pleasant Grove. He had been sick for a long time with the chronic diarrhea and I guess some scurvy. He lived much longer than any of us expected. He was reduced to a mere skeleton. It is no infrequent occurrence to hear the death march four or five times a day. There, I hear it now. One of Company H in our regiment died yesterday and they are burying him now. He was one of their best men so the officers of the company say. He was a Swede a very stout hearty man had been sick but a short time. He was taken to the hospital one day and died the next. There it is, the stout and robust are taken and the lingering invalid left to wear away his existence. This is the only man Company H has buried for a long time. The commander of our Brigade, Col. Williamson of the Fourth Iowa Infantry says we have fewer sick men and more men to die than any other regiment in the Brigade. Since General Osterhaus has taken command of our Division we have to drill more can be more particular in every respect than when Steele commanded. Guards must have their brass scoured their clothes neat and their shoes blackened when they appear at Guard Mounting. We have already had Division Drill one day and Brigade Drill one day. We have inspection once a week by a staff officer and Sunday mornings by Company commanders. Besides this we are required to drill two hours per day at 5 1/2 o'clock. So we are not idle always. We have but little to do on Sundays. Inspection at 9:00 AM drill parade in the evening.

It is still pretty hot but the boys that were home on furlough say that we have no weather as hot as it was in Iowa when they were home. This is true every summer. The heat here is scarcely ever greater here than in the North; but the heat is constant here and lasts longer. This is the reason it is more prickly here; so at least our Surgeon Dr. Allen says. And he has a good deal of experience in this climate, as he was surgeon in the First Iowa Cavalry before becoming connected with this 30th Iowa Infantry.

I want you to tell Jenny and Louie when you see them that I am getting a little mad at them for not writing. I am not very mad yet; but there's no telling how mad I will get. Tell Uncle Mathias Ware that I am expecting to hear from him. If he has not time he has a daughter that might just as well trouble herself that much as not. But I have run out of anything to write.

    As Ever
    Your Son
    Sam

Letter 9

Camp Wood Mississippi
October 4th 1863

My Dear Parents,

When I wrote last I felt confident that ere this I would be with you. But just as I was about to receive a leave of absence an order was received to the effect that no more leaves of absence or furloughs would be granted at present, the division being under marching orders. We received orders one evening, I do not remember the exact date, to be at the railroad by 6:00 next day and went there promptly. We lay there however until six in the evening. I guess there was some misunderstanding and that 6 PM was intended instead of 6 AM. That evening or rather night we reached Vicksburg and went aboard the steamer Thos. E. Tutt and next day went on our way up the river. We were four days reaching Memphis - lay their all-day - saw the boys of the 20th Iowa cavalry except Lieut. Bandy is all that we knew of them. They look as if they had never been sick. We reached Corinth Wednesday evening and came to our present camp next day. We are about two miles and a half from Corinth on a high piece of ground with good water convenient. I can see no reasons why this is not a very healthy location. It seems altogether uncertain whether we stay here long or not. I am rather inclined to the opinion that we will remain sometime and I believe it is the general opinion. If so I may yet get to make you a short visit. Lt. Col. Roberts has been released from arrest without trial and we're expecting Capt. Creighton to be served the same way. I hope he may be released immediately. We are talking of putting up a brick chimney to our tent. It is quite cold at night and a fire would not be out of the way. Martin Luther got his baking out to camp yesterday and will soon supply us with soft bread. He seems to be very well. I have completely escaped the fever and am as well as I ever was in my life. We have here 23 men present in Company C and two of these are sick. I think we will recruit four in health here. I have not heard from David for a long time. I do not know how to direct letters to him. I understand the 14th is yet at Columbus, Kentucky. Is David in the hospital yet? Please tell me how to direct his letters if you know. Joe Pengh met us at Memphis. He was very well. I received fathers present and it came in good time, for I had just lost my pocket handkerchief. It seems to me a long time since I received a letter from home. I can account for this. You were expecting me home and thought it useless to write.

This is Sunday morning and it looks very much like Sundays at home. I should like to go to church but no such thing is known in our regiment. How I wish we could have a good chaplain. Henry Simmons of the first Alabama regiment (colored) called to see us the other day. He seems very pleased with his new position as captain of a nigger company. I think from what he said that he is expecting a promotion. I have met several old acquaintances here. But I have other duties and must stop. As Ever

Your Son
Samuel B. Heizer

Letter 10

Camp 30th Iowa Infantry
15 miles West of Tuscumbia
Alabama, Oct. 22, 1863

My Dear Parents,

You will doubtless have heard of the fight in which our regiment was engaged yesterday and in which we lost our noble Col. Torrance and five others killed 22 wounded before this reaches you. Our Company had three men wounded Alanzo B. Larkin lost his right leg below the knee. George

W. Anderson wounded in the shoulder. Thomas Bell slightly wounded in the hand flesh wound. Several of the boys got bullet holes through their cloths. David Carmean got a shot through his pants leg but it did not touch his leg. He said for me to say he was all right. He has been quite well lately. Martin Luther is very well. Proctor and Creighton reached camp while we were out yesterday and Proctor delivered the two pairs of socks and black berries for Luther and me. They came in good time. My feet were wet and dry pair of socks in a dry pair of shoes felt very comfortable. You speak of me having the diarrhea. I have not had it since Proctor started home. I have fattened up since he left till now I am quite fleshy and feel bully.

But I must hasten.
    As Ever
    Your son
    Sam

P.S. In the fight yesterday the Rebs got on three sides of us and we had to fall back. We were within 40 yards of the rebs before we knew it.

    Your Son Sam

Letter 11

Camp 30th Iowa infantry
Chattanooga, Tennessee

December 2nd 1863

My Dear Sister,
    I was a little surprised yesterday or rather this morning when I received a letter from you. The mail came last night, but I did not get the letter until this morning. I have not written home for a good while and it was a good deal longer

time that I did not hear from home. About a week ago I was going to write home but I felt so unwell that I gave it up and told Luther to say in his letter to his wife that I had the ague. I did not have the ague a few days before and I felt very much like having it then but I did not quite make out to shake. Since then I have been with the Company all the time. We have been in two fights since then. In both of them there were a good many killed and wounded. But I was not touched in either although in the last one the bullets came closer than I ever heard them before. David Carmean was laying just to my right behind the same log that I was, for the balls flew so thick and fast at us that we all lay behind logs, trees, stumps, and whatever else we could find and Dave said he saw the splinters fly from the log nearly all the time. Now I know they came close to me for the log was scarcely as thick as my body. I thought certain my time had come at last. But the bullets kept flying and I was not touched. One Regiment close to ours lost all their officers but two in the 7th Ohio.

Our Company was very fortunate. We had but one man touched and he was only scratched on his head enough to bring and numb his hand for two or three hours. Our two fights were on Mission Ridge Tennessee, and White Oak Ridge, Georgia. We did not get to fight at Lookout Mountain because they put us on a little hill to guard a battery that was throwing shells at the rebels. We had a good view of the fight. We can see the rebels running and our men running after them. We felt very glad when we saw our men driving them. They kept us beside the battery all day and then ordered us up the mountain. It did not seem very far up. But we had to stop three or four times to rest before we got to the top. The mountain is nearly one-half mile high. But I must end in a hurry for it is getting late and cold.

I believe the boys are all well except Newton McBride and William Darlington. They are both with the company. The rebels are driven from this part of the country and we expect to start for Huntsville tomorrow. I may not I get a chance to write for some time. If I do have a chance I will write. So "Good Night".

    Your Brother
    Sam

Whenever you want a letter write to me. Tell Father and Mother I will try and write soon. I am looking for a letter from Joe.
    Sam

Letter 12

Woodville, Alabama
December 31st 1863

My Dear

    It is a stormy night. The chilling blasts sweep through the tree tops. The rainfalls at regular intervals and all outdoor is dark and gloomy. Above the howling of the wind I hear music as if it were from a camp meeting. It is the many voices of soldiers who seemed unusually happy tonight. I know not what it is that has aroused them so, unless it is the presence of Mrs. M. E. Woods of Jefferson County with a supply of provisions for the 30th. This good old lady has visited us before and made our hearts glad with her good things and her good humor. This time she has brought quite a supply, for which we are grateful. We are always glad to see friends from the North but more especially when they bring us delicacies which cannot be obtained here. We have been very busy for a few days back. At the end of this month we have to make out muster rolls, monthly returns of company and alterations in the company. Quarterly returns of deceased soldiers and of men joining the company, return of clothing census and Garrison equipment and return of ordnance and ordnance stores and today the last of the month to be mustered. All day it was stormy and most of the time raining. The muster in the storm was not very pleasant, but it was a military necessity. We're still in this miserable camp in Woodville and it does not seem to improve. It was muddy when we came here and the rains do not make it any better. I do wish they would move us to a better place. Our adjutant says we are only waiting until it clears up to move into winter quarters a few miles farther on. I wish they would move on. I would almost as soon be on the march in such weather as this as to lay in our present camp.

I received a letter from home yesterday and also a Hawk Eye in which was a list of killed and wounded in our regiment. So my folks know I am safe. The letter was from Joe and he had not heard from me since the battle although it was nearly a month after the fight. I can't account for so great a delay of the mails. I wrote soon after the battle and should have had an answer before the date of his. My letters from the North generally come in a few days. In fact letters have been received from Iowa four days after they were mailed. I should have answers to several letters to you since the fight; but as yet I have received none. I have not been remiss in writing when it was in my power to do it. I have written at least three or four times and it seems to me oftener; but it is of no avail to complain if Uncle Sam does not bring my mail in a reasonable length of time. I will only have to wait.

It is turning quite cold and I would not be surprised if it would freeze up tonight. I suppose it would seem strange to me to go north and see snow. I did think I would get to go during holidays. But I was doomed to disappointment and I have almost given up the notion. It seems in some Corps officers and men can go whenever they desire while in ours there is scarcely even a chance; but then there is something to prevent me from going. I have been in command of Company F of our regiment since we left Bridgeport till today. I was really glad to be released from responsibility of the company by the return of Lieut. Bence of that company. I had no trouble with the company but it is much more pleasant for every company to have its own officers. But the drums are beating for roll call. I must a stop here. I am impatient to hear from you. Brother Mark returned to regiment today.

As I ever hope to be I am yours.
Sam

Letter 13

Camp Proclamation
Paint Rock River
Alabama: January 6, 1863 (Note: actual date, 1864)

My Dear Father and Mother,

As our Sergeant Major McCeasy starts for home tomorrow morning I thought I would not be a miss to send a letter by him, although it is but a short time since I wrote home. I wish I could be the bearer of my own message as McCeasy is of his but some of the officers have not as yet received leaves of absence and it is yet uncertain whether they will receive any or not. If any are granted I will probably be one of the number of fortunate ones. As this is altogether uncertain and as it would be several days before we could leave at any rate a few lines may not be a miss. If I do get to visit my friends I shall not be able to be at home more than five or six days. For you know I have another friend that I must see and I will just have more than ten days to spend in Iowa. But I need not count the days until I know whether I can get off or not. If I do not to you may send by McCeasy what postage stamps you have not already mailed of the money I sent you a few days ago. You need not delay writing either for I ought to get an answer to this before time for me to start if I am so fortunate as to get off. Martin Luther and I are both very well as McCeasy can tell you. It is not worthwhile for me to write much for he can tell you all you want to know. If I do not get home before McCeasy starts for the regiment I wish you would buy for me

a first-rate gold pen, pencil and case, such a one as you think would be of most service, without respect of cost and send it by him and I will send you the money by mail whatever it is. Such a thing is next to impossible to get here and the cost unreasonable, five or six dollars and not anything extra at that. I suppose such an article as I would like would cost four and a half or five in Burlington. Mark said you wanted to know if I wanted any shirts such as those you sent him. There are just such as I would like. Such a shirt would cost here at least five dollars. I paid five for one not long ago. But I need not write anymore McCeasy will tell you all the news.
    Your son, Sam

Letter 14

Camp Proclamation
Paint Rock River Alabama
January 9th 1864

My Dear Mother

    I wrote home but a day or two ago and sent it by Jim McCray. Yes I thought I could not spend an hour more pleasantly than by writing again. Our mails have been very small lately and as we are laying in camp with but little to do and nothing, almost, to read we get lonesome and almost homesick. I always did love to write letters as you will remember. You recollect father used to think I wrote too much. I acknowledge I did write more than was really necessary; but then it was a great pleasure to me and I acquired habit that has stuck with me ever since to write to my friends, when I can, very often. If it does you as much good, and I have no doubt that it does, I say if it does you as much good to read letters as it does me you'll not be sorry that I acquired the habit. When the mail is not detained, as I fear is now, we have a good deal of reading. Capt. Creighton takes his church paper "The Religious Telescope" published at Dayton, Ohio, an excellent paper which I get to read, I take the Weekly Hawk Eye and then we get a daily from the news box nearly every day. These with what letters we get and occasionally a magazine supply us pretty well. I intend taking "The Evangelist" as soon as you send me a copy so that I can find out where to write for it. I think then I will have about as much reading matter as we can well manage. The boys have about completed their winter quarters. They have built log shelters which will be very warm. Captain and I have not yet, and we are not quite certain that we will build a house. Our tent is very good and we have built a fireplace and chimney that makes it very comfortable. It is not, however, as warm as a shelter would be and we may yet build one. It has been quite cold here for a few days, as cold, the citizens say, as it has been for several years. The Third Division of our army Corps has been passing here. They are on the way to Huntsville. It must be pretty cold traveling. The soldier gets a custom to a great many things that seem pretty hard and they do not seem to him so very hard after all, that is after they are done. I do think though they might let us rest during the cold weather. There is a rumor in camp that our division will not remain here much longer. I hope it may turn out to be untrue for although our camp is a pretty rough place, we are now pretty well fixed and I think this a pretty healthy location. However if it is necessary I am ready to leave at anytime. We are no better than others moving and we may as well go as they.

 Capt. Creighton and I went to a farmhouse not far from our camp, yesterday, to see if we could get some washing done. The family consisted of an old lady who had been a widow many years and her daughter in law of hers whose husband was killed in Virginia in the rebel service, and two children. This is but one instance of the effect of the rebellion. Here is an old widow; her widowed daughter in law and too little fatherless children, dependent on Uncle Sam for a livelihood. The man they say and I am inclined to believe them for they seem to be honest and religious, was not at first in favor of secession and when the secession ordinance was submitted to the people he voted against it, but afterwards when the rebel government passed their conscription act, to avoid the draft he volunteered in the rebel service and was killed in a battle in Virginia. I had some doubts as to the truth of the story when Captain took up the oldest child, a girl of about seven years and asked her if she liked the union soldiers. She did not seem to understand him, the old lady then told him to ask her if she liked the Yankees and she would know what he meant. When she heard this question she looked up at him and then hid her eyes behind her hands, as much as to say no. I thought this a pretty good test but said nothing lest I should get the old ladies ill will and fail in getting my washing done. These people have some very strange ideas. Captain inquired if when the war began she had any idea the Northern Army would ever get so far South. She said she did. That she thought the Scripture taught it. For she said the Scripture said "should pass over". We did not ask her for an explanation; but supposed she referred to the destroying Angel for we could think of nothing else that she could have meant. I really pity these poor folks. For I believe they were inclined to do the right at first and were really loyal to the Government at Washington, but that they were partly persuaded and partly scared into loyalty to the Rebels Authority. How these people are to subsist when the Union Army is withdrawn is a mystery to me. I suppose there are hundreds of thousands of women and children in the Confederacy in as destitute circumstances as these are. I am very sure of one thing. I shall be very glad the war, the cause of so much distress both North and South shall cease, the rebels having first submitted to the rightful authority. For this let us continue to labor, and pray fervently.

In my letter I sent with McCray I said something about a gold pen that I wanted father to send me. I believe I said to send a pen, pencil and case. I have changed my mind a little since I wrote. I believe I would prefer a gold pen with an ebony holder in a neat case without the pencil. I like a common lead pencil much better than a pencil in a pen holder. Send then the gold pen ebony holder and case. You wrote that you wanted me to send you another photograph. For there is no chance now to get one and I think when I do get it I will not look sickly. For I have a much healthier look now than when the one you have was taken. I had not been rid of the ague very long and then we had just finished a very hard march and I was pretty well worn out. But must stop.
 As Ever,
 Your Loving Son Sam

Letter 15

Headquarters C. C. 30th Iowa Infantry
Camp Proclamation
January 28, 1864

My Dear Mother
 I received a letter from you a few days ago. But as I had received one from Joe the day before and an answer was due to his first I thought best to defer an answer to yours a few days. I suppose that long before this reaches you Luther will be with you if he is not now. I hope his stay may be pleasant to him and all his and my friends. I have been very well since he left. I was weighed day before yesterday and weighed 165 pounds, more than I remember of ever weighing before in my life. I was on Picket yesterday and last night. Today I was with the company on the battalion drill. We are having very fine weather. It seems like spring in Iowa would. Drill brings a free perspiration and I think it is just what we need. Some

of the boys are out playing ball this afternoon. They are very lively. Two officers and form and started from our regiment for Davenport today recruits said to be there for regiment. I hope they will get 300 on Monday. We lack that many of having a full regiment. We have a little over 300 at present. Mark can tell you just how many there are by the number of rations he had to issue when he was here. However we have about as many as most of the regiments have. I told Mark when he left that he might bring the things that I sent by McCray. We are looking for the paymaster now and as soon as we are paid off I can send the money for them and some beside. I have about all the clothing I shall want for a good while and I will need but little money beside where I will have to pay for board. Yet I always like to keep more on hand than I expect to need, lest something might happen that I could not foresee and I might need it. Here after I shall try to save what I can reasonably; for I see that if I ever do get home I will need all I can get. I think very likely I shall want to attend college about three years and that will cost at least $200 a year beside what I can make during vacations. Such are my intentions providing I live and keep my health; but even if I do not so I will need it. I never yet was in a situation where I did not want money and I hope I never will in this world. As far as getting a leave of absence is concerned that he is remote. I cannot get it. I applied but the application was disapproved at Corps Headquarters. If anybody wants to see me they will have to come to the 30th Iowa for I expect to be with it while the war lasts if I live.

    But it is time for Dress Parade and I must stop.
        I am as ever your affectionate son,
        Sam Brown
        Co. C. 30th Iowa via Nashville, Tennessee
        P.S. Direct as usual. Sam

Letter 16

Camp 30th Iowa Infantry Volunteers
Paint Rock River Alabama
February 4, 1864

My Dear Parents

    I received a letter from Martin Luther today. I have not heard from home for several days and was getting restless fearing something evil had happened. I thought that in all probability he would be on his way to the regiment when this reached you and so concluded not to write to him. I also by the same mail today received, Tom Cambello's letter which it seems it was sent to Kossuth and there remailed by Martin Luther. I hope you and Luther and all interested will enjoy Brothers visit home. I very much regret that it is impossible for me to visit my friends this winter and in all probability I shall not be able to visit you till the expiration of my term of service. The only thing that I know of now that would take me home is sickness that would require a change of climate and a surgeon's certificate to the fact. But from present indications I am not to have any such misfortune. My health continues excellent and three letters this evening revived my spirits, which were getting pretty low, greatly. No one but a soldier knows how much good it does a soldier to get letters from the dear ones at home. I know how anxious friends at home are to hear from their sons and brothers in the Army for I was at home when the battle of Fort Donaldson was fought and I remember how anxious we all were to hear from the 14th Iowa. At such a time a letter from the Army is a greater satisfaction to friends than a letter from home would be to the soldier! But at any other time I think the soldier is just as anxious to hear as is the friend in what one of our Captains calls "God's Country". I like that name. It sounds so sweet and it is so expressive. Then it is the land of our birth, the land that we call "home sweet home." The land where our the loved ones dwell, yes the land for whose sacred institutions and rights and star spangled banner we are ready to sacrifice all that we have and are not withholding even our life's blood. How exceedingly small the sacrifices if it would bring about the desired result. With all these associations clinging to it how appropriately it is called "God's Country". But enough of this for this time.

We are still laying in camp idle and unemployed except that we go on guard about every third day and send out a Scouting or foraging party every five days. You may think this pretty hard duty, but it is better than being on the march every day as we were last fall. Lt. Col. Roberts is out on a scouting expedition now with a detail from our regiment and several others. Our Regiment furnished 25 men. The whole party were mounted on mules and armed in their usual way with their guns (Springfield Rifled Musket). What success they have had we do not know. Lt. Col. Roberts is the right sort of a man for such business. He is quick, brave, and judicious. If in anything he errs it is being too brave. I have looked for him to be shot down in every fight we have been engaged in so far. But he seems to bear a charmed life. I do not like many of the Cols. ways, but no man can ever truthfully charge him with cowardice in the face of the enemy. I do think he exposes himself too much, but yet he is ever careful to protect his men.

We still have Battalion Drill. We learned two new movements today. By Thursday I heard from some source or other that the 14th Iowa had gone south from Columbus, Kentucky. I don't know whether it is the case or not. If you know I wish you would write in your next letter. I am anxious to hear from Dave. He owes me a letter now and I am looking by every mail for letter from him.

But I must bid you "good night"
I am as Ever,
    Your Affectionate Son
    Sam B. Heizer

Letter 17

Camp Proclamation
Paint Rock River Alabama
February 7th 1864

My Dear Parents

    I received a letter from mother today and with it a letter written by William S. Brown to her Jan. 23rd, which I return with this. I am still enjoying excellent health and let me tell you we are just about as comfortable as we would be at home. To be sure we are deprived of many luxuries and pleasures of society and religious privileges; but as far as bodily comfort is concerned we are very well off. This is a Sunday night. It has been a very pleasant day. We do not have preaching in our regiment. As you are aware, we have not had a chaplain since we left Young's Point Louisiana. However Captain and I sang several hymns and I read some in the Testament during the day and besides we did what we could not well be avoided of business for the company. This evening we received orders to have the payrolls for November and December signed and witnessed and to hand them in to Headquarters before 8 o'clock in the morning. This is a very good sign that we will be paid in a few days. I hope we may be paid soon.

    I shall look for Martin Luther about Thursday. I hope he will get here before we are paid; for I think you'll want the money. However if he does not I can accommodate him with enough to do him till the next payday and not send so much home. I hope to be able to send $100 this time. Lt. Col. Roberts is absent from the regiment in command of a detail from the Brigade guarding the Tennessee River for about 20 miles. There are some rebels on the other side and he is watching them. I understand there has a force crossed the Tennessee above and another below him and you may not be surprised if you hear of a lot of rebels gobbled somewhere near Guntersville, Alabama. If it be true that our forces have crossed both above and below and I think there cannot be doubt of it, the rebels will stand a poor chance to escape.

I received a letter from Oami Heizer today. She spoke of you all being at their house not long ago. She says she likes to teach school but likes to stay at home better. I shall not probably have the opportunity of seeing those cousins of mine in Ohio Regiments. I think we will not be near enough to each other to visit. But it is getting late and I am sleepy. You must excuse me if I do not write long letters. I shall try and make up in numbers what I lack in length. Continue to write often. I hear there is a great revival going on at Kingston. How is it? But I must tell you "goodnight". You need not look for me for 18 months yet. I do not expect to get a leave of absence till my time is out.

>I am as ever
>Your Affectionate Son
>Sam B. Heizer

Letter 18

Saturday Night
February 14th 1864

My Dear Sister

Martin Luther brought me a letter from you and one from Joseph. I thought it would answer yours tonight and Joe's in a few days, so that you might not get more than one letter from me at a time and you'd hear from me oftener. Mark and I are both very well. I believe he is writing to Sister Sally tonight. There is but little news that I have to write. I received your picture and the article's mother sent me. I was really glad to get your likeness. I can see it looks some like you but I do not think it a very good picture. I would like to have the picture of the whole family but suppose I cannot get them. The song book Mark brought has some very beautiful songs in it. I have learned several of them. Mark and I sing them together. We are having very good times, plenty to eat, plenty to wear, good comfortable quarters, not much duty to do and an abundance of reading.

We are expecting to be paid off in a few days. The paymaster sent for the payrolls about a week ago. Money is about the only thing we lack now. I hawk a newspaper every day and once in a while a magazine. This takes money. I do not doubt but that I spend some money that I should not, but then I did not go into the Army to make money, but to fight.

We have several rebel prisoners here. Yesterday one of them got away. I think he ought to have been hung. They say he helped to hang a union surgeon. I think such men ought to be hung as soon as they are caught.

I am sleepy and tired and must stop writing. So "Good Night".

Your Brother Sam

Letter 19

Paint Rock Creek Alabama
February 22nd 1864

My Dear Parents,

Yours of the 14th I received by today's mail. It was just seven days on the way a little better than a great many of my letters make. Capt. Creighton and I took a walk down the RR about two miles this evening and when we got back had a talk with some of the boys and now since roll call I have seated myself to converse with you. We're having most delightful weather nowadays, just liked the first part of May and Iowa. I shall soon be looking for flowers and then I intend to send some to you in a letter. We are having very light duty now and the health of the regiment is remarkably good. Mark's and my own health are excellent. I am having an easier time now than I have had since I enlisted. Col. Roberts has detailed me as recruiting officer for the regiment to remain with the regiment. The idea is to get recruits from the country here. Our Alabamian came in a few days ago and enlisted in Co. G. I would not be surprised if we were to get 15 or 20 recruits from this state. Yet we may not yet another man.

Today you know is Washington's birthday. Well, they (the big officers of the 13th Army Corps) had a high time at Huntsville today. So I am told at least. At Woodville about one mile from here the First Iowa Battery fired a salute of 21 guns in honor of the day. But it is of more consequence to me that it is my own birthday. Today I am, well you know how many years of age, 22 the way I count it. There has not been anything of much importance taken place here since I wrote last. I understand that the regiments of our army corps that went to Chattanooga not long ago have been ordered back to Woodville, Larkinsville and Scottsboro the places they left. These places are all on the railroad between here and Stevenson. We have a great many rumors as to our proceedings during the summer, but nothing reliable. I would just as soon think that we would remain here for months yet as any where else. The most welcome report is that the paymaster will soon be here. Let him come. It looks to me as if the war would wind up during the 12 months to come. I have never, as you know, been very hopeful of a speedy termination of the war. Yet a starving army and a starving people cannot always hold out. We had preaching in camp last night. It was the first since Mr. Kephant preached for us at Bridgeport. The orderly Sergeant of Company E preached for us last night. He is a Methodist. He is a very fair young man. There is some talk of making him chaplain. I do not know whether they will or not. I do wish we could have a real good chaplain. I feel more at home when I can occasionally hear a sermon. There is a rumor in camp that we are going to have a chance to reenlist. If it be true I think nearly every man will reenlist. But I hardly credit the report.

I am sorry that Sassieh Carmean is so unwell. I was thinking of writing her letter but I believe she never asked me to write. I guess I will not trouble her unless she asks it. General Osterhaus is again with us. We are all glad to see him.

    Very Truly Your Son
    Sam

Letter 20

Paint Rock River Alabama
February 25th 1864

My Dear Father

It is but a few days since I wrote you. Yet they say circumstances alter cases. Our regiment received pay last evening and this morning as I am sending a part of my wages home by express I thought it would be proper to write you concerning it forthwith. I only spend $50. I might spend more, but Mark was some in-debt on account of his furlough and I loaned him some. If I had that I could send it. But I thought it my duty to accommodate him. I do not expect to expend all I keep. But I think it best to keep a little extra in case of sickness or wound or if we should go into the field again and not be paid for three or four months. The money was sent in care of W.W. Harper Burlington and by calling on him you can get it. Mark and I are both very well. No news of importance.

    Your Son Sam

Letter 21

Headquarters Co. C. 30th Iowa Infantry Volunteers
Camp Proclamation
Woodville, Alabama
March 21st 1864

My Dear Mother

    Yours of the 9th I received yesterday and intended to have answered last night, but for some reason I do not remember what I failed to do so and tonight shall attempt to atone for the delay by writing more than I would have done last night and some things I could not have written then. I was over to the 25th Iowa this afternoon in company with Corporal Ganaway of our company to hear Reverend Baird a Cumberland Presbyterian minister from Burlington, Iowa preach. I had heard him once before, on the occasion of the presentation applied to Co. E. 1st Iowa. He made but a short address then, but said enough to satisfy me that he was a pretty well educated man. I was not disappointed in my expectations today for he preached us a very plain logical (?) address. It was a real treat. We scarcely ever have preaching in our regiment and when we do have it it does not amount to very much. Then too, his being from Burlington made me feel almost as if I were listening to one from home. If folks only knew how much good it does us to see old familiar faces from the North I do believe more of our friends would visit us. Mr. Baird came to take to Iowa the body of one of the 25th Iowa. He was, however, from what I can learn made his visit one of usefulness. He seems to be an earnest Christian. Mr. Proctor received a letter from his son Columbus in the 14th Iowa yesterday, from which I understand that David is all right. He did not mention any fighting. I guess the 14th Iowa did not have any fighting all the time they were out on the expedition.

    I cannot agree with you in regard to the President's call for volunteers. I don't believe it would pay to put into service

500,000. I think it would be more than a quartermaster's and commissioners departments could provide for, when the limited transportation furnished by the railroads leading to the important points in the South is considered. I do not think it would be policy to call for more men than to be used with effect. Every unnecessary expense should be avoided by the government. I do not want the government to be so extravagant as to become bankrupt at the end of the war and greenbacks to be good for nothing. But I have little fear of anything of the kind as long as the administration continues to act as wisely as it has done thus far in the war. But I suppose it is not worthwhile or profitable for me to discuss political questions and so I leave the subject trusting to "Uncle Abe" and the constitution for the result. And it shall ever be my prayer that God would direct our rulers in the right path and overrule all things for his glory and the nation's good.

My recruiting business has played out and I am doing duty with the company as before. So you need not trouble yourself about my coming to Kossuth for recruits. We have two officers and several men on the recruiting service, absent from the regiment now and no more will be sent out while they are away and it is not likely that there will be any sent after the return.

I am glad to hear of Harriet Carmean's improved health. It seems Aunt Eulium has a great deal of trouble. I think John Harper and Uncle Foster if they are such warlike men had better, go South. I think we could find plenty of shooting to do here and in a much better cause that I suppose either of them has now. Then they would greatly relieve their families by putting and end to family quarreling with rebels. It is strange what fools some men will make of themselves. Now I do not know anything about the cause of their trouble and don't care much more than I know. Now maybe I have spoken thoughtlessly, I want justice done to both. Whichever is to be blamed I want to hear of having been punished and that forthwith. I am very well satisfied with the investment father made of my money an so is Martin Luther. I shall send some more about $100 next payday, which I am perfectly willing to have used in the same way. I suppose Uncle Henry is very well satisfied with the trade in as much as he has made a good thing by it. I hope Uncle Henry will be more successful than in Kansas. It would be a good thing for Kossuth and the neighborhood if the Covenants would buy the Free Church and then the Free Church would give the money toward building a Church. The new school folks could raise as much and with this and the Free Church's money a splendid building could be erected and furnished sufficient for both churches and then it would be an easy thing to support a first-rate preacher and much more good to be done than at present. So at least it appears to me. I would like to see it tried.

There seems to be apprehensions by General Osterhaus of an attack upon us. We have orders to be ready to fall in at a moment's warning and the First Iowa Battery have one of their cannon loaded with a blank cartridge to give the alarm in case of an attack. I hope our fears may not be realized. But in case of an attack we are prepared to give the rebs as warm reception as they could ask. But I am not troubled much about this. I trust the enemy will not be so impudent as to attack us in our present position. Mr. Hay's fault that you speak of: that he is a strong war man is a fault that I cordially approve. But I must bid you "Good Night."

> As Ever
> Your Affectionate Son
> Sam

Letter 22

Camp Proclamation
Woodville, Alabama
March 28th 1864

My Dear Parents

    I received your letter today and with it a letter from David which I have copied as you requested and send you the copy with this. I don't know whether you can read the copy any better than the original, I tried to put it all on two pages so that I would not have to pay double postage by sending two sheets. Mark and I are both very well. It is raining today. It is pretty muddy. I understand our army corps has marching orders. We have not been officially notified of the fact and it may prove a false report. You need not tell me anything about the widow Hill and Joe Pilling but let me know all the other views of interest. I can't see that there is anything that would interest you that I could write. Whenever anything occurs that is of importance I will let you know.

    I am
    Your Affectionate Son
    Sam

Letter 23

Camp 14th Iowa near Vicksburg
March 5th 1864

Dear Father, Mother

    To all whom it may concern thank God we are back once more to America, after a March of over 400 miles through the heart of the Confederacy. We have marched to the heart of Mississippi to the line of Alabama. I am well and hearty as ever. I was fat as a pig, dirty and lousy. We left Vicksburg on the 3rd of February marched to near Black River. The 4th took up our line of march, crossed Black River on pontoons, skirmishing commenced and kept up all day went into camp 25 miles east of Black River. The 5th marched at an early hour skirmishing all day and went into camp six miles of Jackson. The 6th struck tents, on our march passed through Jackson and left in ashes as we did all the rest of the towns behind. The 7th marched through a barren country, plenty of swamps. The 8th we marched all day, passed the 17th corps at dark and marched seven miles of swamp, went into camp about 2 o'clock marched 27 miles. The 9th took up our line of march at an early hour advanced seven miles and went into camp weary most of the boys washing their feet and socks. The 10th marched at 6 o'clock passed through Hillsboro at 9 o'clock. Got plenty of tobacco in Hillsboro and left town in ashes. The 11th again on the march at an early hour, camped within 25 miles of Meridian. Passed through Decatur. The 13th on the march and at noon came up with the enemy's rear guard; heavy skirmishing kept up all afternoon and a running fight. It was the rebs falling trees on our way but we clearing them up as fast. They also burned bridges, several prisoners taken and some lost a few killed and wounded. The 14th reached Meridian at 4:00 PM and went into camp. The 15th layed in camp until two o'clock, struck tents and went two miles west of town and went into camp, rained all day. The 16th at daybreak on the march out on the Southern Mississippi railroad, laid off our blankets and went to work tearing and burning railroad. Had a slight skirmish. At night went back to camp. The 17th again tearing railroad three of C Company taken prisoner. The 18th laying in camp today with no rations, but plenty to eat, a hog last night and this morning that cost $300 but a few days before. The 19th still in camped yet no rations, but have honey fresh and salt meat cornbread, potatoes, and all that could be desired. The 20th struck camps, on the march, marched on the union railroad. The 21st up at four and on the march at sunrise - march 21 miles and in camp at night. The 22nd again on the march. Washington's birthday and Jeff Davis's inaugural. The 23rd again on the march through Hillsboro. The 24th marched 15 miles and went into camp at night. The 25th March 4 miles and wait for the 17th to cross the pontoons - lay in the road all night. The 26th on the march, passed through Canton and camp one mile of town. The prettiest town I ever saw. The 27th lay in camp all-day, at evening 16 men detailed to grind corn. I stand guard all-night while others are grinding. The 28th lay in camp all day, at eve tear up railroad. The 29th last eve ordered out on picket for our regiment. 1st March, strike tents and start on our march. March 18 miles through rain and mud, pass-through Livingston, sleep on a bed worth $100 of cotton. The 2nd are attacked in the rear after marching about six miles. The 3rd marched all day, passed through Brownsville, coming to the Jackson Road 1 1/2 o'clock and cross Black River about sunset and camp about dark on this side. The 4th start for Vicksburg 15 miles, arrived at our old camp about one hour of sunset meet the new recruits, whole look well. Ed Ware has the mumps. Can't write anymore, have to go on guard, will stay here but a few days when we will go on the boats for where I can't say but expect Texas. Thank God I never had better health in my life and stood the march, never rode a step. The boys all stood it well.

>From your affectionate son
>D. B. H. (Note: This letter was written by Sam's brother as mentioned in Sam's letter of March 28, 1864. The signature should be D. B. H.)

Letter 24

Woodville, Alabama
May 1st 1864

My Dear Father and Mother

One week ago yesterday our regiment received orders to proceed immediately to Trianna, Alabama, and in the afternoon we were put aboard the cars and arrived at Huntsville, Alabama the same night. Our wagon train was started from Woodville by the wagon road. Sunday morning after having spent the night in the rain getting pretty wet so we started for Trianna - which we reached in the evening having marched about 19 miles during the day. We remained until day before yesterday when we received orders to pack up and march to Woodville. We started about sunset and marched about nine miles that night getting to Madison Station about 10 PM just in time to escape a soaking rainstorm. We set out the next morning (yesterday) after having been mustered for pay and came 23 miles. This morning we again set out and reached Woodville this evening a short time before sunset. We found our Division had left for Chattanooga. We received orders to follow them and will be on our way early tomorrow morning. Mark and I are both very well. I shall probably not have a chance to write soon again. Rumor says we are to guard the railroad; that our Division will guard the road from Chattanooga to Stevenson. I hope it will prove true. But I must bid you "goodnight."

    Your Son
    Sam

Letter 25

Kingston, Georgia
May 20th 1864

My Dear Parents

    As I have a chance to write this morning I thought it would be well to let you know I'm not dead, wounded, or taken prisoner although I have been pretty badly scared. I was in a fight at Resaca three days. On the evening of the 2nd day, May 14th, we charged nearly a half-mile and drove the enemy about a quarter. So you see we are now at Kingston. Mark and I are both pretty well. I have a bad cold. I have not time to give you the killed and wounded; you will get that. But I must stop here.

    Your Son Sam

Letter 26

Camp 30th Iowa
July 7th 1864

My Dear Parents,

    I have put a few moments to write and can write but little. I am pretty well. Mark is well. We are now near the Chattahoochee River. The enemy it appears are nearly all across the river and what remains are getting across as fast as possible. Our company has had but two wounded since I wrote last, Thomas Davis and Milton Reuste. They are both doing well at last accounts. I have not read a letter from home for some time. You must be busy now harvesting and have some excuse for not writing. Yet I do not feel satisfied unless I hear from home. You may think me negligent. I write as often as I can. I shall write as I have opportunity. The mail has to be at headquarters at (words obscured). It's near that now. I must close.

    Your affectionate Son
    Sam B. Heizer

Letter 27

In The Field
before Atlanta GA
August 5th 1864

My Dear Sister Irene,

    I received a letter from you a few days ago if I am not mistaken and now as I have a place fixed and time to write I will answer it. I am not, as often I could wish able to answer letters, yet I think I do as well if not better than the folks at home, when our chances are compared. But it is not worth my while to fill up a sheet with this kind of talk. Since I wrote last I have been in several fights. But so far I have not been touched by the rebs. I hope I shall be as fortunate in the future, and get to see home once more. We are now lying in reserve in the second line of breastworks. Our duty is very light. We have no skirmishing to do. The last time we had any duty to do we were on picket in the rear. We did not see any rebels and I think there were none there. But then we have to look out for them in every direction so as not to let them come up when we are not looking for them and capture some of us or some of our rations or destroy the railroad behind us.

    There has been some pretty hard fighting in this neighborhood lately but we have been fortunate enough not to be present at any of it since the 28th of July. That day we had but one man hurt slightly. Our regiment has been very fortunate since we left Kennesaw Mountain. We have had but three severely wounded during the last month.

We drew new clothes day before yesterday which makes quite an improvement in our looks. Some of us, and I was one, were very ragged and dirty. It is impossible to keep pantaloons clean situated, as we are, where we can have but one pair and always on the move. I got a new suit all round except socks. I had a good supply of them before. I believe I am in want of but one thing now and that is postage. I wish father would send me 25 or 30 stamps. I have no money or I would send it to pay for the stamps. There is a report that the paymasters are coming to pay us off in a few days. Then I will have some money to send home, but more than I have sent, heretofore altogether. But I had better not count my money yet. It may prove a mistake about the paymasters. I hope it is not a mistake.

Mark was in camp today. He is quite well. I heard from Dave Carmean a day or two ago. He was then doing very well. I hope he will get well soon, for he is a brave soldier. One of my company died at Marietta a few days ago. He was taken suddenly ill, taken to the hospital and died the next morning. His name was William F. Long.

I shall look for an answer from you very soon. Don't forget to write your affectionate brother.

You may call me Capt. Sam B. Heizer

Letter 28

One-half mile in Rear of 30th Iowa
Near Atlanta, Georgia
August 17th 1864

My Dear Parents

As you see I am not on duty with the regiment. For several days I have been troubled with a very severe headache caused Dr. Rogers says by being overheated last summer while in the Vicksburg campaign. I got permission of the Colonel and Dr. to go to the rear to where the Dr. stays for a few days to see if rest and quiet would not stop my complaint. I came out yesterday in the forenoon. My head troubles me but very little when I keep cool and quiet; but heat or noise give me great pain and sometimes it seems as if my head would burst. In other respects I am quite well. I hope that a week's rest will be of great advantage to me. If I do not get better by that time I think very likely I will go to a hospital where I can have more attention. Since I wrote home last Company C. has had one man killed and one wounded. Our rifle pits until a few days ago were in plain view of the rebels skirmish pits at a distance of about 150 yards. Both these men were shot in our rifle pits. John W. Howell was wounded by a ball striking along on our breastwork and glancing. E. T. Huleing was shot across the back near the kidneys while digging in our rifle pit and died almost instantly. Co. B.'s first lieutenant was shot through the head by stray ball the other day and died in a short time after. Besides these there have been four in the regiment wounded since I wrote last making seven killed and wounded during the last week or two.

When I heard from David Carmean and a few days ago he was doing fine. He expects to start home in a couple of weeks.

Our company has been unfortunate during the campaign thus far. We started from Paint Rock with 34 men and have lost 13 (11 wounded and two killed); over one-third of the number we started with.

I saw Mark this morning. He seemed very well. The health of the company is as good as could be expected. Some are complaining but none very sick. My headaches and I must stop.

    Ask Ever
    Very Affectionately Your Son Sam

Letter 29

Camp 30th Iowa volunteer Inf.
August 25th 1864

My Dear Father, Mother and Brother

    Brother Mark read a letter from Sallie last night bringing the sad and painful intelligence of the death of our Dear Irene. I was not prepared for such news. I first heard it through Frank Hamilton their regiment having received the mail an hour or two before ours. I could not believe it until Sister Sallie's letter was received. Mark allowed me to read the letter giving the particulars of her sickness and death. It is sad indeed for one so young to be cut off so suddenly, yet we have the consolation that it is God's doing and all he does is right. Were it not for this I would not know where to look for help and consolation in time of trial. I well remember how many hours I have spent singing with her in "the Golden Chair." How when I was a cripple she attended me, how many wearisome hours she shortened by her presence. Oh how I wish I could have seen her before her departure from Earth. I had indeed hoped for this, for her stay with us has seemed, for longtime seemed doubtful. But now she is gone and we shall see her no more in this life. Yet we all I doubt not hope to meet her departed spirit in the land of the blest. I know I shall miss her "when this cruel war is over". I hope to see that happy time as you do now. I shall miss her smiling face and greeting and that glad meeting will be mingled with sorrow and I shall go to the lonely graveyard and see only the mound and the marble slab. I cannot see Irene. It seems I cannot get her out of my mind. If I could but weep it seems to me it would be some relief, but that relief I am deprived. You know how it is with me. But I must hasten. Our regiment I have just heard is under marching orders and I cannot write much. I wrote so short note the time ago that I have but little news. I have improved in health and am going back to the regiment this evening. We are now again on the second line; our skirmishes have driven back the rebel skirmishes and the second Brigade of our division having thrown up a line of works in our front, which they now occupy. I am expecting a lively time shortly. Everything seems to indicate a moment of great importance. What will be done I of course do not know. Mark and Pengh(?) have just now come in with rations of some kind I guess forage for the mules and horses.

Here I must stop short off.

    As Ever Very Affectionately
    Your Son
    Sam B. Heizer

If you have an extra photograph of Irene please send it to me. It seems to me I heard you had some.

Letter 30

East Point GA
September 15th 1864

My Dear Parents,

I received Mother's letter in answer to one I wrote some time ago to our Dear Irene. I little thought before writing it that she would be laid in the silent grave before it would be answered. But so it is, we never know when we write that the one to whom we write will be among the living when the letter is read or numbered with those who have gone to the spirit land. But we must trust our dear Irene had gone to the blessed clime where pain and sin and sorrow cease and where all are pure and happy. I shall not again in this world join her in singing those sweet songs we used to sing together but I hope to see her again in that better land.

Luther Vannice heard from home last night of his Father's death. He feels very badly and I feel sorry for him. It seems all have their trials and this is his just now.

Mother, I am afraid, has two good an opinion of me better than I have myself. I wish I were as good as I should be. I do try to live aright, but I fear I have come far short of my knowledge. As for friends I do not expect ever to lack them. As long as a man is a man he will have plenty of friends and I expect ever to be a man.

You want to know whether to send Irene's photograph or keep it for me. I wish you to send it to me. I have a very good place to keep it. Mark says he will not send for his if I get mine, for it will do us both while we are absent. Be sure to send it in your next letter.

I received the stamps Father sent. They came in very good time as stamps always do. They are a thing it is almost impossible to get here and I have to use a great many. All official letters except those to Washington require prepayment of postage and some of them two, and in this way a good many are consumed. I can generally get paper and envelopes. I have a very good supply now. I have a good deal to do now. All the back returns since we started on the campaign except one were to be made out and a great many other things. Clearing off Camp was a big job but that is done and we have gotten tents and are pretty well fixed for soldiers. We had inspection of everything today. The inspecting officer gave us great praise for our industry. He said we have the best kept guns in the Brigade.

I received a letter from David the same time I received yours. They had just got back from Oxford, Mississippi the day before he wrote. His letter was dated Sept. 1st. He says that if ever he goes into the service again it will be in the Artillery. I think his decision very good. I believe the artillery service the nicest of any army service. I have my doubts whether he ever enlists again but it would not surprise me much if he did. It is hard for a young man to stay at home while the war goes on even if he has spent three years in the Army and has seen hard service. I think it best to let him decide for himself whether he stays at home or not. He is the one who ought to know his duty if anyone does.

But I must go to bed so "Good Night."
    Very Affectionately
    Your Son Sam B. Heizer
    Direct as usual.

Letter 31

Camp Detachment Department of the Tennessee
Chattanooga, Tennessee
October 18th 1864

My Dear Father, Mother and Brother,

As you see I have not yet reached the regiment. It seems very uncertain when I will be able to do it. I reached this place Oct. 10 and the next day got on a train going south supposing I would be able to join the regiment in 24 hours, but upon arriving at Dalton we learned that the rebels had attacked Resaca and that it would be unsafe to proceed further. So the train backed up to Dalton where we remained until the next day when General Schofield came down from Knoxville and learning that the rebels were advancing on the place he ordered the three trains in the place back to Cleveland, Tennessee and from there back to Chattanooga where we arrived next morning. We got away from Dalton just in time for as soon as we left the enemy came into town and the garrison surrendered and as we were unarmed we would've been unable to render any aid to the garrison. Upon our arrival in Chattanooga the first commander Col. Stanley ordered all officers absent from their commands in the city not on duty here to report to headquarters and there gave orders to organize all the troops in the same situation as ourselves and Col. Roberts was assigned to the commander of this detachment. I acted adjutant for the Col.

until he was able to get a suitable lieutenant and now I have nothing to do. We are all longing to get to our regiments. There are several officers and men here of my acquaintance four of my own regiment so that I do not lack company. I have been in excellent health since leaving home. Have not heard from the regiment since I left it.

I must bid you Good Evening.

    Yours Very Truly
    Sam B. Heizer

Letter 32

Camp Detachments Depart of the Tenn.
Chattanooga, Tennessee Oct. 24th 1864

My Dear Father, Mother and Brother,

I have as yet been unable to join my regiment and am still on duty in this camp. I have however heard from the regiment two or three times. When I heard last all of my company were well. The regiment had not been in a fight since I left and from what I can learn I think they will not be in as much as Hood seems to be trying to make his escape southward and is now probably farther south than our army is prepared to follow him. I do not think Sherman can follow him very far because his teams are so worn out that they can do but little and without provisions an army can do nothing but starve and provisions sufficient to subsist an army are not to be found in the country after Hood's army has passed through. Rumors as to the destination of the Army of the Tennessee are very conflicting so that an opinion can hardly be formed and would be worthless when formed. So I shall not tell you when or where I will join my command simply because I have no idea when or where I will be able to join it. I am very anxious to get to the old 30th and shall attempt to get to it as soon as I think it worthwhile to try. I have not heard from home since Col. Roberts left and do not expect to till I reach the regiment. Then I expect to get a great stack of letters. Direct all your letters as you have heretofore. I took a stroll the other day in company with Captains Smith and Walkins of the 30th Iowa and a Captain of the 31st Iowa all of whom are in the same situation as myself. We got a pass from General Steedman commanding the district of the Etowah to go beyond the picket lines and made a visit to Lookout Mountain which is distant from our camp about a mile and a half. From the foot of the mountain it appears a short distance to the top but after climbing halfway up it looked about as far off as at the beginning. We ascended from the North and passing over a part of the ground on which the battle of Lookout Mountain took place last autumn. A part of the way we went up by an old wagon road that winds like a serpent up the mountain but thinking that too crooked we took to the foot paths which although much steeper in as much as they go more directly up the mountain is somewhat short shorter route. A little more than halfway up is a house or once was a house for it is now torn down, and orchard and a field. There is a spring close by. This was once a place of resort for Southern aristocrats but now entirely deserted. We rested here a few minutes and then continued the ascent which now was even more difficult than before. We however kept on resting occasionally until we came to the foot of a ledge of rocks that borders the summit for miles in either direction. This ledge we ascended by means of ladders and took our position on the point of the ledge fronting Chattanooga. From this point we have an extensive view. As far as the eye can reach in every direction are mountains. On the right is Chattanooga Valley and a creek of the same name. Beyond that is Mission Ridge were last fall from our present position could be seen through a spyglass the vast armies of Grant and Bragg in deadly conflict. On the right center is Chattanooga with its government depots and workshops. In front is the Tennessee River winding among the mountains and hills. It seems as if nature had tried to hinder its progress by throwing mountains in its way. Yet it manages to pass all these and is lost in the far west behind the mountains and still flows on. To our left is Lookout Valley and a creek of the same name. Beyond this creek the 15th Army Corps last autumn found General Hooker fortified on a range of hills running parallel with Lookout Mountain. Beneath our feet around the side of the mountain Hooker's 11th and 12th corps reinforced by Osterhaus's Division of the 15th corps swept and the rebels fled in confusion like clouds before the wind. And here I heard and joined in the shouts of the victors and heard the groans of the wounded and dying. Lookout itself lies very nearly north and south the sides converging so as to form an acute angle at the north end the summit bordered as I have said by a ledge of rocks for miles, from 30 to 60 feet in height so that for two or three miles back the mountain is quite narrow. From this point we wandered back to Summertown passing on our way several fortifications not now used among them a large unfinished blockhouse. We passed to one dwelling house in which was a family. On inquiring of the man how he managed to make a living he told us by farming; but how or when he got his crop I could not discover. He said there was about 100 acres of farming land on this end of the mountain but for my own use I would rather have my mother's garden. I believe I could live better off it.

Summertown was formerly quite a resort for travelers but now it is principally occupied by troops and the officer's hospital. There are at present but few patients in this hospital about 30 I was told by the surgeon. I think it a very foolish notion of some very foolish surgeon locating this hospital here. For although the place is very healthy when a man becomes acclimated to change I think from the valleys to the region of the clouds while a man is in poor health, injurious as men who have been patients here testify.

After getting some refreshments at a shop nearby and resting a while we began the descent by a turnpike road, which although much longer than the way by which we came is not near so steep. We arrived in camp in time and will prepare for a hearty supper feeling well paid for our tramp although we did not have time to visit some of the most interesting parts of the mountain: Rock City, Lulu Falls and the lake.

    Very Affectionately Your
    Son Sam B. Heizer

Letter 33

Kingston Georgia
October 27th 1864

My Dear Parents

    I have not yet reached the regiment and will not probably for about three days yet. Our battalion was detailed to guard a corps of Paymasters to Atlanta. We left Chattanooga Tuesday morning on the train and reached Dalton in the evening. Lay in the railroad depot overnight. Left Dalton about eight next morning and marched to the Resaca. The railroad between Dalton and Tilton was not all rebuilt. I understood that five miles were yet to be built. That I guess will be completed today. This morning we got on the cars at Resaca and reached Kingston about noon. Here Col. Roberts kindly relieved me and my lieutenant and consented to let us go on to the regiment while he and the battalion went on to Atlanta. As there is no train going to Rome this afternoon I thought had a good opportunity to write home. I am stopping with Rev. Mr. Kephart. I am very anxious to get out. I am very well. Mr. Kephart is well. I have Col. Roberts's baggage in charge, which will trouble me some. I heard from Mr. Emhart that Yellow Springs Iowa had the Monument which I was very glad to hear. I think if every Iowan in the state does as much towards putting down the rebellion as Yellow Springs, Iowa will not be behind.

I must tell you of a very sad accident that occurred the day before we left Chattanooga. While I was looking at a revolver belonging to Capt. Croso of our regiment I raised the hammer and in letting it down it slipped from my fingers and the load was discharged wounding two men of my company in the leg. I saw the men in the hospital when their wounds were dressed. They were not dangerous. This is the first time I even fired a revolver and I think it the last. Corporal Cross says he never saw a man worse scared than I was. I believe him for I feared that one was killed. By the way I gave my pocket-handkerchiefs to bind up their wounds and am left with out any. Please send me some good ones by mail. Enclosed find the money to pay for them.

    Very Affectionately Your Son
    Sam B. Heizer

Letter 34

Camp 30th Iowa Volunteers Infantry
Near Savannah, Georgia
December 18th 1864

My Dear Father, Mother and Brothers

You may be assured I was glad when our first mail for several weeks came to us day before yesterday. We are now where we had little idea we would be when we enlisted. We are all well and I am happy to say not a man in company "C" has been unable to march during the campaign. Our rations are pretty short just now but this will be the case but a few days. Before I go further I must give you some idea of our march. During nearly all the march we have had very favorable weather. I reached the regiment from home on the 31st day of October just

28 days after leaving you. I was then at Cave Springs 16 miles from Rome. From there we went to Vinings Station 14 miles north of Atlanta. On Saturday Nov. 12th we were engaged destroying railroad northward thus cutting us off from all our friends and all of supplies except what we had with us. The next day we began the march southward and resting one day near Atlanta proceeded on our way towards Macon. On the evening of November 21st we reached the Macon and Savannah railroad rear. Resting here the next day the rebels attacked the 2nd Brigade of our division and were driven back with a loss of about 1000 killed, wounded and prisoners. The 2nd Brigade lost but a few. The next day November 23rd we set out for Savannah. On Saturday November 26 we crossed the Oconee River. Sunday November 27 our Brigade destroyed nearly three miles of railroad and marched about 25 miles the hardest days work of the campaign. This day for the first time on the campaign I saw General Sherman. He had on a Colonel's coat without shoulder straps and was talking with another man by the roadside near his headquarters. From this time on we passed through pine forests and swamps making about fifteen miles per day passing down the right side of the Ogeechee River to Wright Bridge where on the seventh of December our Brigade crossed and moved out to the railroad three miles where we met the 4th Division under General Cose. This day the 4th division had a skirmish with the rebs and one skirmisher captured one Rebel with a blue coat on which Col. Williamson of the 4th Iowa commanding our Brigade made him exchange with a Negro for a gray jacket. Bully for him. If the soldiers had been permitted they would have killed him on the spot. This night as our wagons and pack mules were left on the other side of the river we were a little short of rations I had now. But some of the boys gave me my supper and the next morning our pack mules were up again. That night while posting pickets, as I was Brigade Officer of the day I in company with the Officer of the day before with the guard just relieved summoned a squad of about 50 Gamblers. But as the

guard was insufficient most of them escaped. What we still held we turned over to the Brigade Headquarters where they were put under guard and sent to the commanding officers of the regiments to be disposed of by them as they thought best. Gambling has become very common among the soldiers since they were paid off at Vinings Station and the evil has become so great that General Woods commanding our Division has ordered that all men found gambling shall have their money appropriated to the hospital fund and themselves and all who were even looking on whether engaged in the game or not put to work on the fortifications under fire of the enemy. I hope this order may have the desired effect. But to continue my story. We recrossed the Ogeechee and marched down the west side to the mouth of the canal running to Savannah and 16 miles from the place. Here we crossed the river and marched out on the towpath of the canal to within about six miles of the city. Since there we have moved around to the right and are now about eight miles from the city of Savannah. As you have heard when this reaches you the 2nd Division of our Corps under General Hazen charged and took Fort McAllister at the head of Ossibow Sound and at the mouth of the Ogeechee River opening our communications with the rest of the world by way of the sea. This was done Tuesday Dec. 13th. Everything that we get will here after come to us in this way. I have but little news to write aside from our march and as I have written that I will close.

I send you and address of Major General Kennards. You may judge of his character by his address. He is considered by good men the Heaveluck of our army. I wish no better Department Commander. He appears to be a very pious man.

Yours Truly
Sam B. Heizer

Direct your letters as follows putting nothing more on them.
   Captain S. B. Heizer
   Co. C. 30th Iowa
   1st Division 15th Army Corps

Letter 35

Savannah, Georgia
December 27th 1864

My Dear Mattie

    I very much regret to that I cannot spend the Holy days with you; but since this is impossible I am trying to spend them to the best advantage. As you have heard some days ago we entered Savannah on the morning of December 21st the enemy having evacuated the place that night previous. Since we entered the city I have been unusually busy making back returns. I have not yet quite completed the task; but tomorrow I think I can finish. Savannah as you know is a large city for the South. Business houses are all closed and consequently things go on very dull and one gets lonely. I think that before long houses will be opened. Our regiment is doing provost guard duty and we're having very good times. Duty is pretty severe, but we do not mind that as long as we have so comfortable a situation. The regiment is camped in a park and the officers are quartered in a four-story brick close by. We have everything necessary convenient. Provisions here have been a little scarce, but a good and abundant supply is being landed today. We have a daily newspaper published in the city. I mailed the first copy to you a few days ago. I sent it simply because it was the first union paper printed in Savannah since the breaking out of the rebellion. I suppose the paper will be continued I hope so for by it we can get later news than from the northern papers. Then to we can get the local news. I do not know whether it is intended we shall remain here during the winter or not. I cannot yet see any indications of a move. It may be to that since we have been detached to do provost guard duty we may be left here when our Division moves. This, however, is altogether uncertain. The troops who garrison Savannah will have a "nice thing". I think it no more than right that we should have a share of the nice things of the

Army and here is the place I would like to have mine located. I have not heard from you or from home since the capture of Savannah and I am very anxiously looking for a letter if not several. I would like to hear if you have received those "views about Chattanooga" and how you like them. They are not as well executed as they might have been; yet they are quite natural. I suppose Chattanooga is considerably changed since I left it. We were constantly at work fortifying the place when I left. We have cheering news from Nashville, Hood's Tennessee Campaign ending just as we of the Army prophesied. We were too well acquainted with the ground over which he had to pass to think that he could be anything else than unsuccessful. The fair prospects of the Rebels are certainly fast waning. One thing is very noticeable the rebels are not so impudent and saucy as they used to be. The tone of the Southerners today in Savannah is milder far than that of the citizens of Nashville and Louisville and Memphis one year ago. I see the mayor of the city has called a meeting of the citizens to make arrangements with the General commanding. The citizens are very civil and I cannot see but they treat soldiers as well as they are treated in the North when they are not just at home. The churches were nearly all full last Sunday the pulpits being filled by their old pastors. How it was at other churches I do not know. But at the Presbyterian Church a large portion of the congregation was soldiers. The minister was very cautious not to say anything disrespectful of the government at Washington. In fact he studiously avoided saying anything concerning our national troubles although his subject -- special provinces, -- would very naturally lead him to them. I do not know whether the present ministers will be allowed to remain. Whether they are or not I suppose will depend altogether in how they conduct themselves and what stand they take of things in regard to questions of national interest. They will doubtless be very careful not to cause a collision with the military authorities.

General Sherman has been reviewing the troops composing this army for the last three days; day before yesterday the

15th corps, yesterday the 17th, today the 14th and tomorrow I believe he is reviewing the 20th Corps. Some think this an indication of an early move. Whether it is or not time will decide. We cannot well move just now for we have not supplies for a campaign. Whether we go on a campaign or not we have about eight months to serve and so it makes but little difference to us whether the 15th Corps rests or not. I hope that by that time the war will end. But it is getting late and my candle is short. Remind Clara of her obligations to me. "Good Night"
    Yours Very Truly
    Direct to
    Sam B. Heizer
    30th Iowa Infantry
    1st Division 15th Army Corps

Letter 36

Camp 30th Iowa
Near Beaufort South Carolina
January 22nd 1865

My Dear Mother

    I hasten to write you a few lines before the mail leaves. We will probably leave here tomorrow and this will be the last opportunity to send from this place. Mark and I are both very well. All the Company are well except Proctor. He was sent to the hospital today. He is not dangerously ill. But as he is getting to be an old man I urged the doctor and he sent him to the hospital at Beaufort. I think he will be back soon. I send you some photographs which I wish you to preserve for me.

    Very Affectionately Your Son Sam

Letter 37

Camp 30th Iowa
Near Beaufort South Carolina
January 28th 1864 (Note: year is 1865)

My Dear Mother

    I send you enclosed the photographs of several members of our regiment, which I wish you to keep for me till I get home. I will send my own soon. I am getting all I can of the officers and others of our regiment. Mark and I are both well. Since I wrote you two or three days ago we have moved about 12 miles. As I wrote but a few days ago I will say no more at present.

    Very Truly Your Son
    Sam B. Heizer

Letter 38

Camp 30th Iowa Infantry
Alexandria VA May 21st 1865

My Dear Brother

    After a hard march of about 30 miles we got into "permanent camp" in plain view of and but a short distance from the city of Alexandria today. We can see the dome of the Capital of the United States and a part of the city of Washington. Next Tuesday begins the greatest review (I suppose) that ever has or ever will take place in this country. I dreaded it I dread any review but this one I must face. We (ie) Sherman's army as you have already learned are to be reviewed on Wednesday the 24th. I hope I may be able to find some excuse for not being on duty that day so that I may escape it. On our way from Richmond we passed Mount Vernon the residence and burial place of General Washington. I was well paid for the march of about five miles out of the way although we didn't get to stop, only march through the grounds and tomb at slow time and then pass on. I would like to see it again when I could have more time to see what is to be seen.

This is Sunday evening. It has been raining almost all day but has ceased now. I have not been very well today. I have a slight attack of diarrhea. I am, however, on duty as officer of the day. The boys are well. Mark and Dave Carmean are very well. All are anxious to be mustered out and paid off and sent home. There is some talk of sending us to Iowa to be paid off. This the soldiers think unfair. It is virtually saying a soldier is incapable of controlling himself. I will keep your money in order that you may not spend it until you get nearer home. This would be very ungrateful in our authorities. If anyone in the world has a right to use his money it is the patriot soldier. Then too many Western soldiers as not wish to go must. Some want to buy government horses or mules to take home with them for farming.

But I must stop.

>Very Truly Yours
>Sam B. Heizer
>I need the stamps you sent yesterday.
>Sam

Part Three

Visual and Supplementary Material

Maps

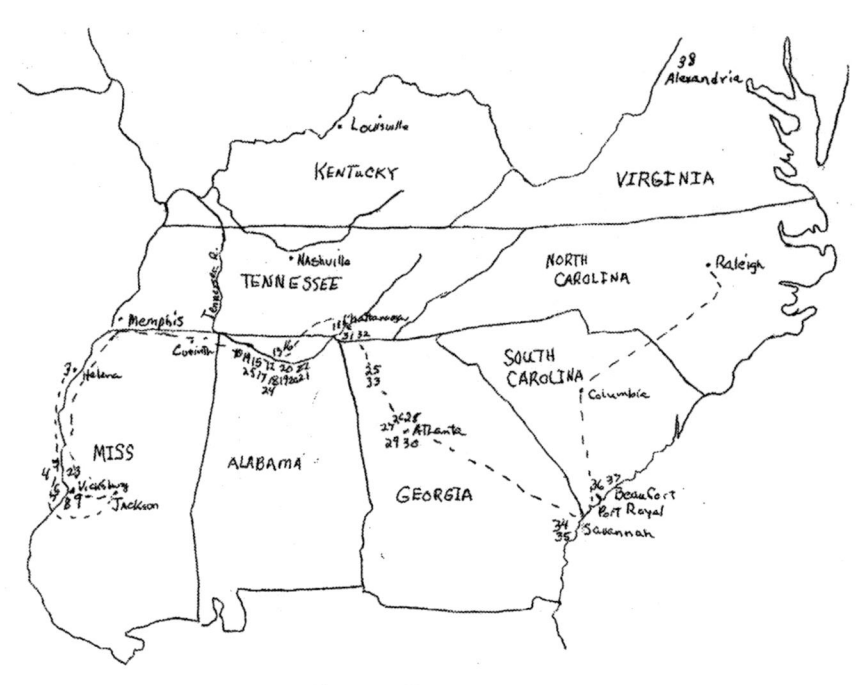

Letter Locations

Sam's Civil War

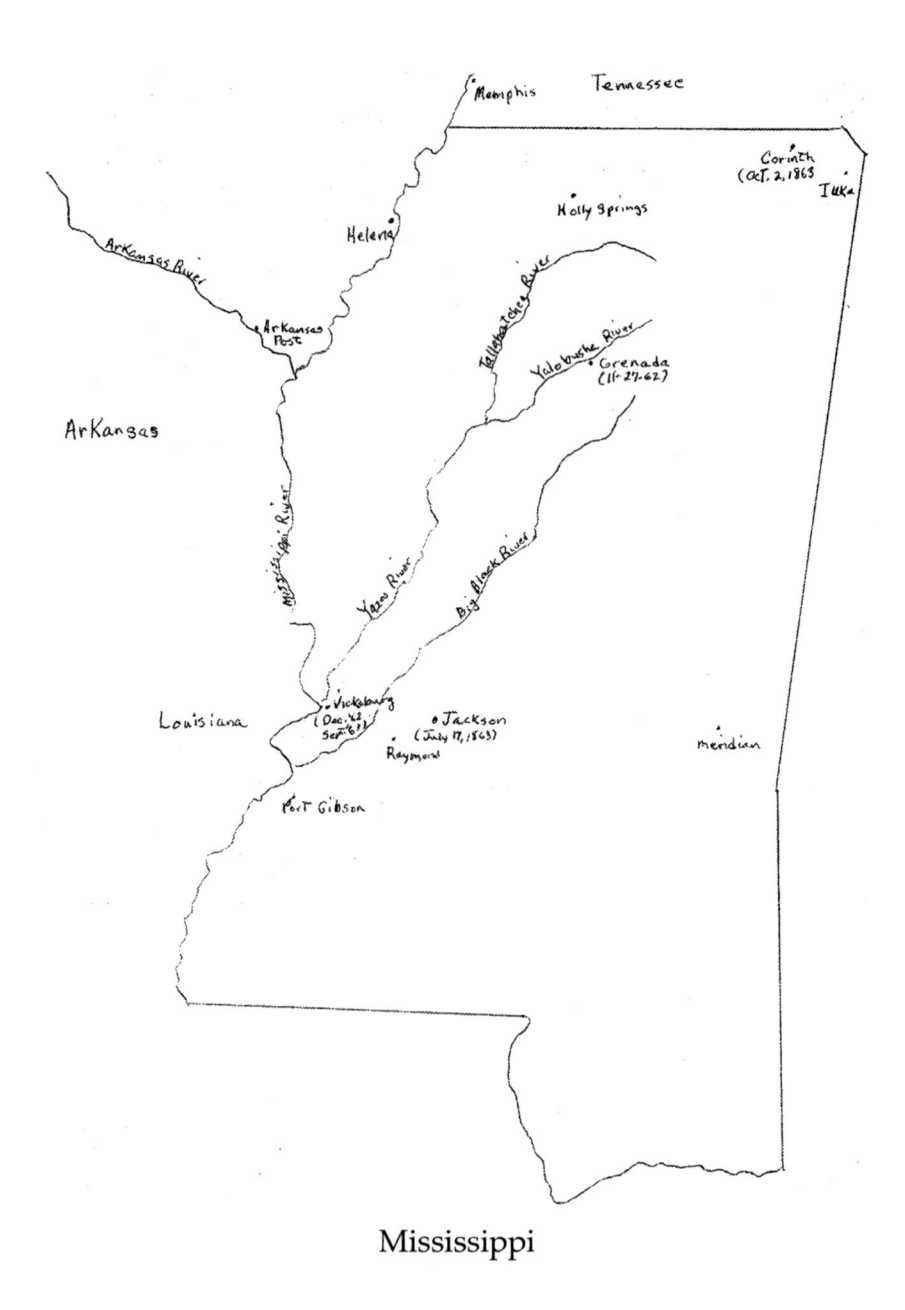

Mississippi

Tennessee-Alabama

Sam's Civil War

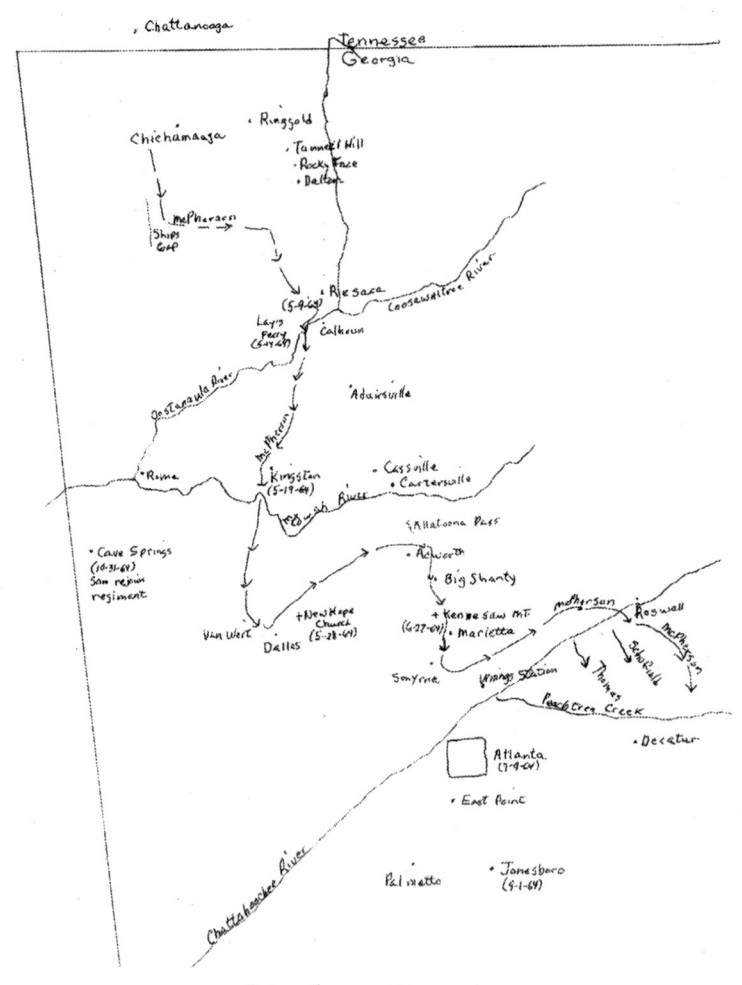

Northern Georgia

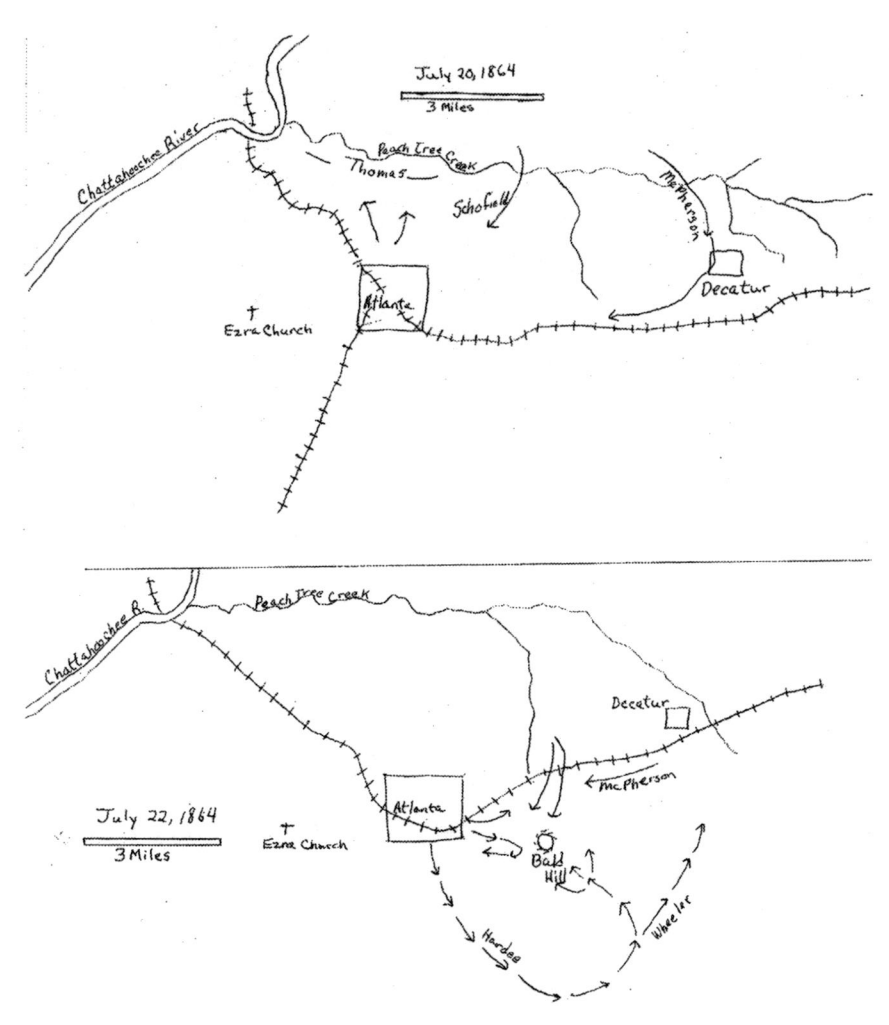

Top: Battle of Peachtree Creek
Bottom: Battle of Atlanta

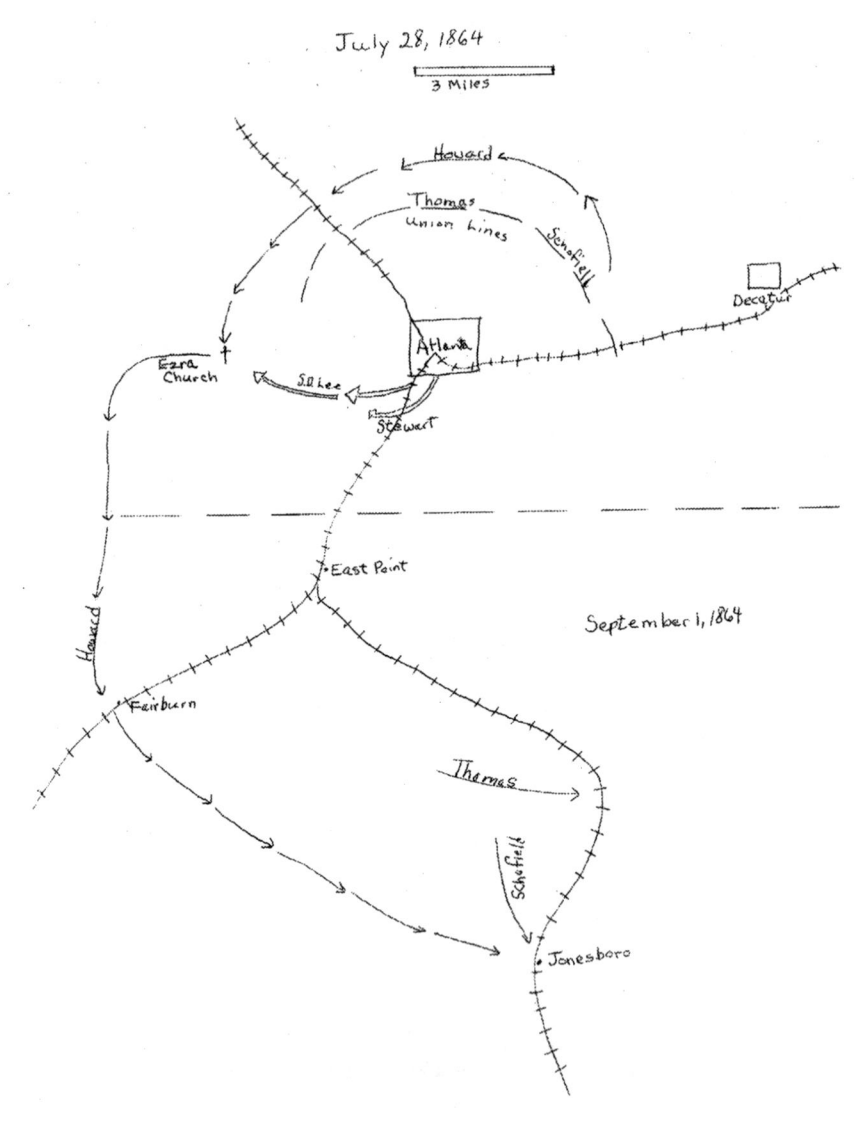

Top: Battle of Ezra Church
Bottom: Battle of Jonesboro

Southern Georgia

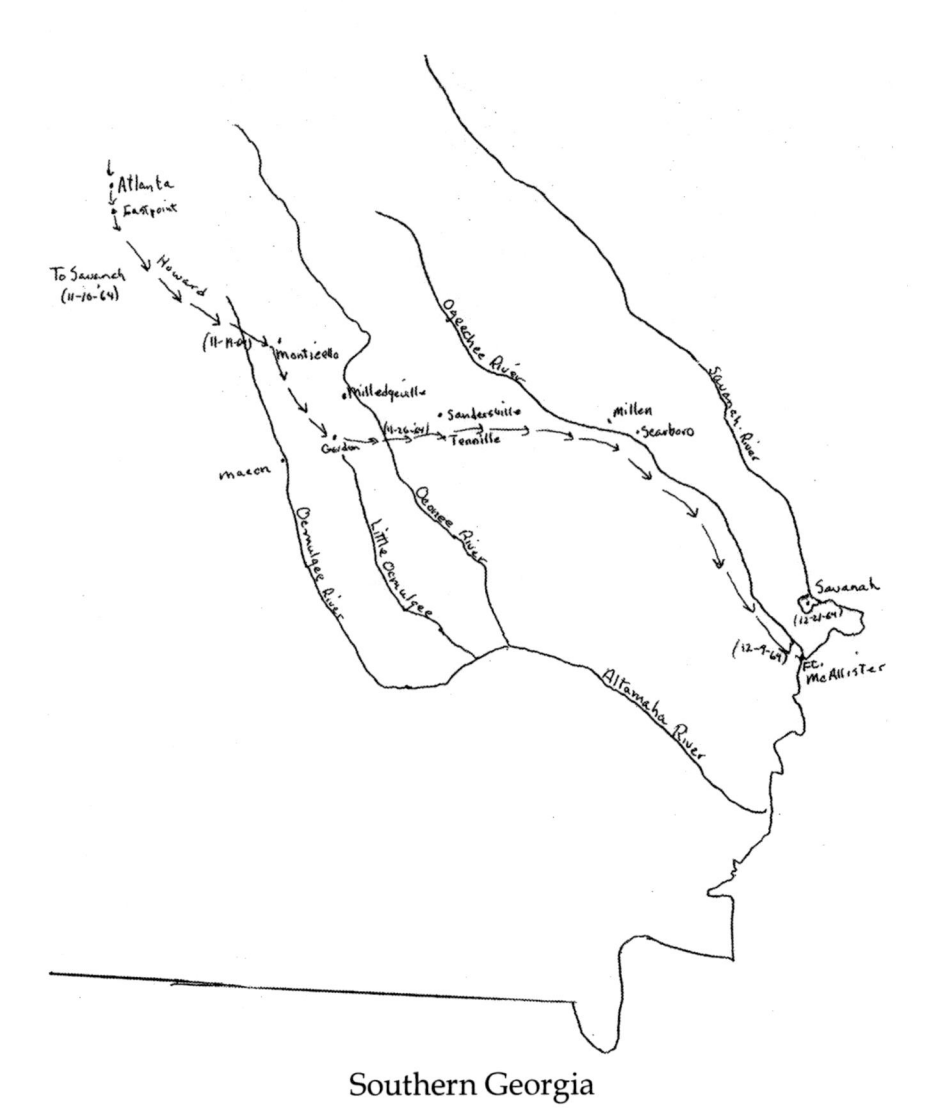

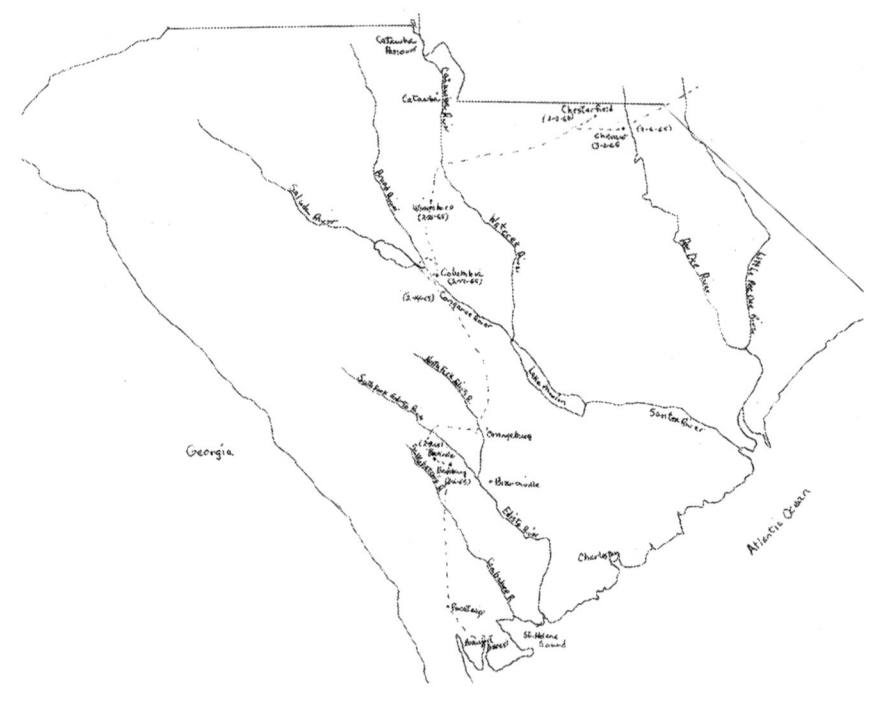

South Carolina

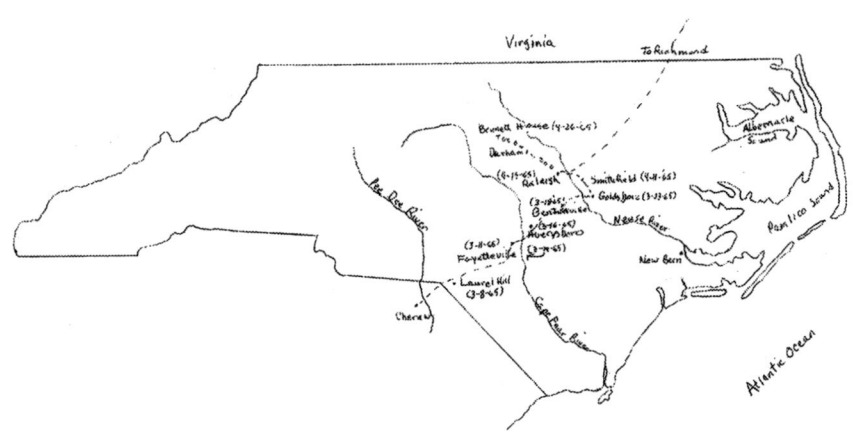

North Carolina

PHOTOGRAPHS

At Home in Mediapolis, Iowa

Martha Canfield Heizer

Sam's Civil War

Sam with Friend

Samuel B. Heizer

Samuel B. Heizer

Samuel B. Heizer

Documents

To all whom it may Concern.

Three pays allowed Aug. 5, 1899
Settlement No. 271691
W. W. Brown
AUDITOR FOR WAR DEPARTMENT

Know ye, That *Samuel B. Heizer*
Private of Captain *George H. Streaper's*
Company, (*B.*) *1st* Regiment of *Iowa Infantry*
VOLUNTEERS, who was enrolled on the *7th* day of *May*
one thousand eight hundred and *sixty one* to serve *3 months* years or
during the war, is hereby **Discharged** from the service of the United States
this to date *20th* day of *August*, 1861, at *St. Louis*
Missouri by reason of *muster out of Company*
(No objection to his being re-enlisted is known to exist.)
Said *Samuel B. Heizer* was born in
in the State of _____ is *49* years of age,
___ feet ___ inches high, ___ complexion, ___ eyes,
___ hair, ___ by occupation, when enrolled, a ___

Given at *Washington D.C.* this *29*___ day of
August 1864.
___
Asst Adjt Genl
Commanding the Regt.

☞ "This sentence will be erased should there be anything in the conduct or physical condition of the soldier rendering him unfit for the Army."
[A. G. O., No. 99.]

5788 B. 1864.

The Commanding Officer of the ... Regiment of Iowa Inf. Vol.

To all who shall see these presents, greeting:

THE STATE OF IOWA

To all to whom these Presents Shall Come Greeting

To all whom it may Concern.

$124.85 pay in allowed Aug 5, 1895
By settlement no. 271691.
W W Brown
AUDITOR FOR WAR DEPARTMENT

JUN 16 1865
U.S. PAYMASTER

Know ye, That Samuel B. Heizer Captain of Captain Company, (C.) 30th Regiment of Iowa Infantry VOLUNTEERS who was enrolled on the 16th day of July one thousand eight hundred and Sixty-four to serve Three years or during the war, is hereby **Discharged** from the service of the United States, this Fifth day of June, 1865, at Washington D.C. by reason of Expiration of Term of service. (No objection to his being re-enlisted is known to exist.)

Said Samuel B. Heizer was born in Ross (co.) in the State of Ohio, is 22 years of age, 6 feet 7/8 inches high, Fair complexion, Brown eyes, Dark hair, and by occupation, when enrolled, a Teacher.

Given at Washington D.C. this Fifth day of June 1865.

A. Roberts
Lt. Col.
Commanding the Reg't.

William L. Alexander
Capt 31 Iowa Infty and

☞ *This sentence will be erased should there be anything in the conduct or physical condition of the soldier rendering him unfit for the Army.*

[A. G. O No 80.]

$124.85 pay thereallowed Aug 5. 1891
by settlement no. 27/691.
W W Brown
AUDITOR FOR WAR DEPARTMENT

To all whom it may Concern

JUN 16a 1865
PAYMASTER U.S.A.

Know ye, That Samuel B. Heizer Captain of Captain Company, (C.) 30th Regiment of Iowa Infantry VOLUNTEERS who was enrolled on the 16th day of July one thousand eight hundred and sixty-four to serve Three years or during the war, is hereby **Discharged** from the service of the United States, this Fifth day of June 1865, at Washington D.C. by reason of Expiration of Term of service. (No objection to his being re-enlisted is known to exist.) Said Samuel B. Heizer was born in Ross Co. in the State of Ohio, is 22 years of age, 6 feet ⅞ inches high, Fair complexion, Brown eyes, Dark hair, and by occupation, when enrolled, a Teacher.

Given at Washington D.C. this Fifth day of June 1865.

A. Roberts
Lt. Col.
Commanding the Reg't.

William L. Alexander
Capt 31 Iowa Infty and

*This sentence will be erased should there be anything in the conduct or physical condition of the soldier rendering him unfit for the Army.
[A. G O No 99.]

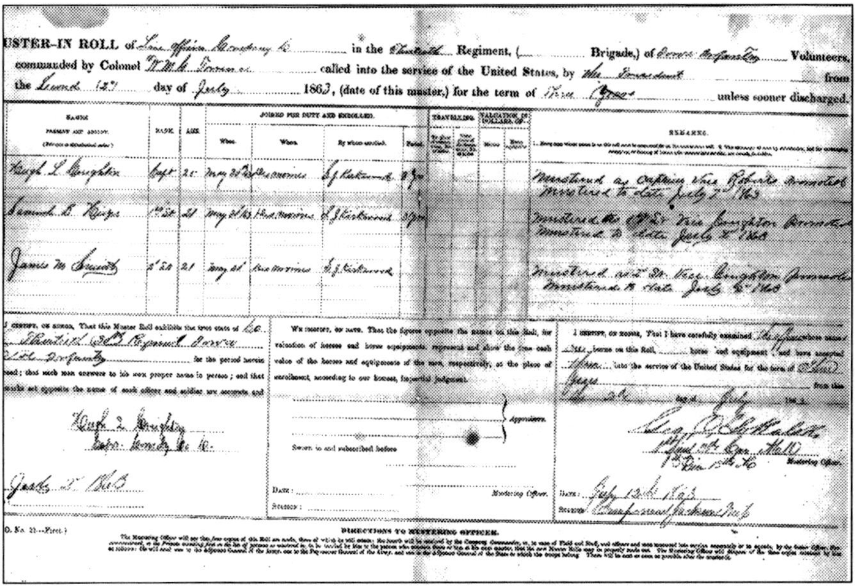

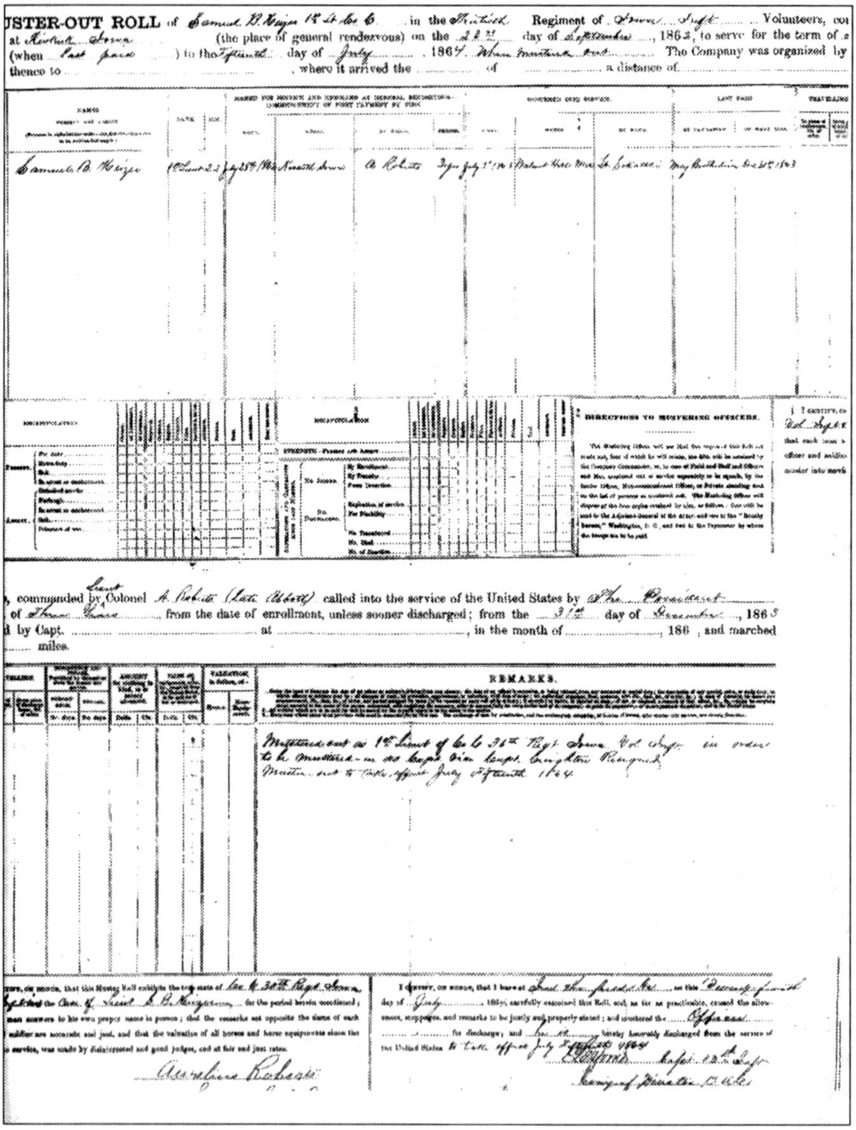
USTER-OUT ROLL of Samuel B. Keizer 1st Lt. Co. C in the Thirtieth Regiment of Iowa Infty Volunteers, co
at Keokuk Iowa (the place of general rendezvous) on the 23rd day of September, 1862, to serve for the term of
(when Last paid) to the Fifteenth day of July, 1864. When mustered out. The Company was organized by
thence to ..., where it arrived the ... of ..., a distance of ...

Samuel B. Keizer | 1st Lieut | 23 | July 28th 1862 | Keokuk Iowa | A. Roberts | 3 yrs | July 1st 1863 | ... | May ... Dec 31st 1863

DIRECTIONS TO MUSTERING OFFICERS.

, commanded by Colonel A. Roberts (Late Abbott) called into the service of the United States by the President
of Three Years from the date of enrollment, unless sooner discharged; from the 31st day of December, 1863
by Capt. ... at ..., in the month of ..., 186 , and marched
... miles.

REMARKS.

Mustered out as 1st Lieut of Co C 30th Regt Iowa Vol Infy in order to be mustered in as Capt. vice Capt. Creighton Resigned.
Muster out to take effect July Fifteenth 1864.

..., on honor, that this Muster Roll exhibits the true state of Co. C 30th Regt. Iowa ... the Case of Lieut S. B. Keizer ... for the period herein mentioned; ... answers to his own proper name in person; that the remarks set opposite the name of each soldier are accurate and just, and that the valuation of all horses and horse equipments since the ... service, was made by disinterested and good judges, and at fair and just rates.

Aurelius Roberts

I certify, on honor, that I have at ... on this ... day of July, 1864, carefully examined this Roll, and, as far as practicable, caused the allowances, stoppages, and remarks to be justly and properly stated; and mustered the Officer ... for discharge; and ... hereby honorably discharged from the service of the United States to take effect July Fifteenth 1864.

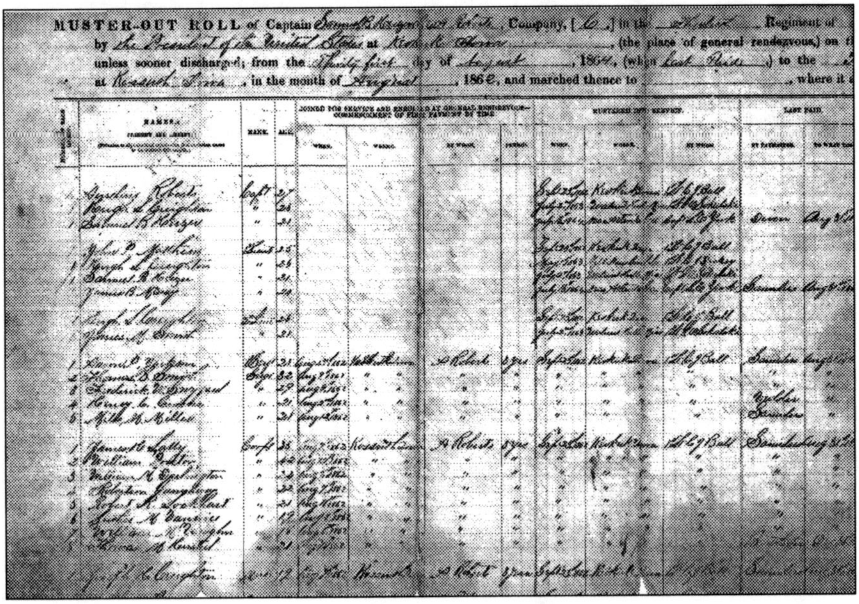
MUSTER-OUT ROLL of Captain ________, Company, [C] in the ________ Regiment of ________ by the President of the United States at Keokuk ________, (the place of general rendezvous,) on th... unless sooner discharged; from the Thirty first day of August, 1864, (when last paid,) to the ... at Kossuth ________, in the month of August, 1862, and marched thence to ________, where it a...

NAMES. | RANK. | AGE. | JOINED FOR SERVICE AND ENROLLED AT GENERAL RENDEZVOUS—COMMENCEMENT OF FIRST PAYMENT BY TIME. | MUSTERED INTO SERVICE. | LAST PAID.

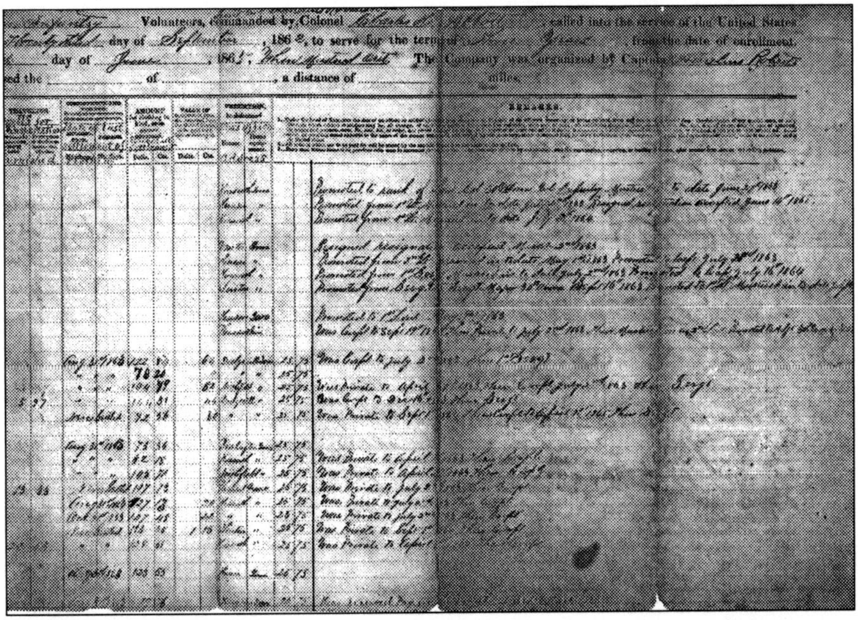
Infantry Volunteers, commanded by Colonel ________, called into the service of the United States ... day of September, 1862, to serve for the term of Three years, from the date of enrollment, ... day of June, 1865, when mustered out. The Company was organized by Captain ________ ... the ________ of ________, a distance of ________ miles.

REMARKS.

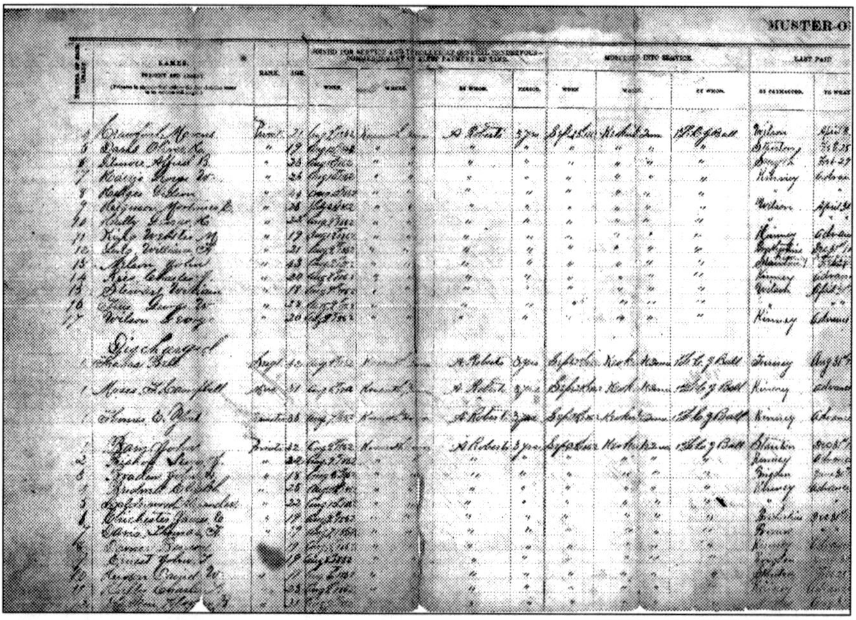
MUSTER-O
NAMES.
RANK.
AGE.
MUSTERED INTO SERVICE.
LAST PAID.
Discharged

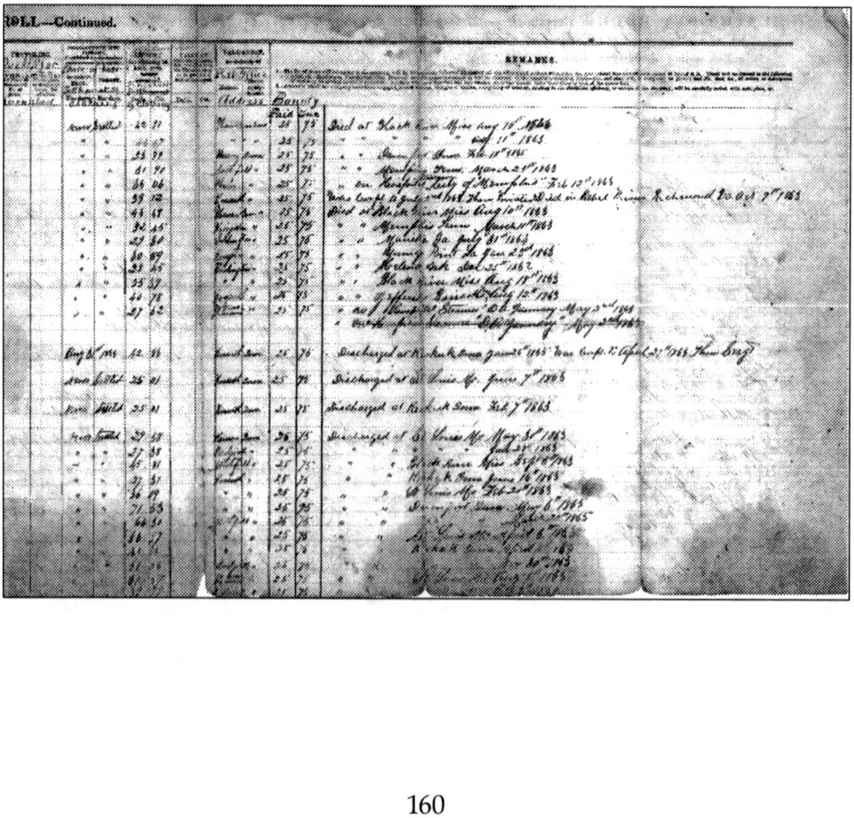
ROLL—Continued.
REMARKS.
Bounty
Died at Black River Miss Aug 10th 1863
Discharged at Keokuk Iowa
Discharged at St Louis Mo. June 7th 1863
Discharged at Keokuk Iowa Feb 7th 1863

LETTER ANALYSIS

Letter 1   Date: June 24, 1862   Location: Iowa City, Iowa

   Officers mentioned:
   Units mentioned:
   Places mentioned:

Letter 2   Date: August 31, 1862   Location: Keokuck, Iowa

   Officers mentioned: Captain Roberts
   Units mentioned: Iowa Co. C., 30th Iowa Volunteers, 36th Iowa, Co. C. of the 30th Regiment, Company A
   Places mentioned:

Letter 3   Date: December 8, 1862   Location: Helena, Arkansas

   Officers mentioned: General Price (C), General Grant, Brigadier General Hovey, Gen. Washburn, General Wyman, Lieutenant Colonel Torrence, Lieutenant Creighton
   Units mentioned: First Iowa Battery, 28th Iowa, 30th Iowa
   Places mentioned: Delta, St. Louis, Benton Barracks, Tallahatchee River, Coldwater River

Letter 4   Date: January 6, 1863   Location: Paint Rock River, Alabama (one mile from Woodville)

Officers mentioned: Sergeant Major McCesay
Units mentioned:
Places mentioned: Burlington

Letter 5   Date: March 2, 1863   Location: Opposite Vicksburg, Mississippi

Officers mentioned: General Grant
Units mentioned: 26th Iowa
Places mentioned: Arkansas River, Arkansas Post, the Canal

Letter 6   Date: April 30, 1863   Location: Millikens Bend, Louisiana

Officers mentioned: Captain Roberts, Major Stanton, General Thayer
Units mentioned: 30th Iowa
Places mentioned: Mississippi River, Keokuk

Letter 7   Date: May 24, 1863   Location: Near Vicksburg, Mississippi

Officers mentioned: General Thayer, Captain Roberts, Lieutenant Col. Torrence
Units mentioned: Co. C.
Places mentioned: Perkins Farm, Aclow, Carthage, Jackson, Mississippi

Letter 8   Date: August 20, 1863   Location: Black River Bridge, Mississippi

Officers mentioned: Captain Creighton
Units mentioned:
Places mentioned:

Letter 9   Date: September 13, 1863   Location: Black River, Mississippi

Officers mentioned: Captain Creighton, Colonel Williamson, General Osterhaus, General Steele
Units mentioned: Company C. 30th Iowa Infantry Volunteers, Company H, 4th Iowa Infantry, 1st Iowa Cavalry
Places mentioned:

Letter 10   Date: October 4, 1863   Location: Camp Wood, Mississippi

Officers mentioned: Lieutenant Colonel Roberts, Captain Creighton
Units mentioned: 20th Iowa Cavalry, Company C. 14th Iowa, First Alabama Regiment
Places mentioned: Vicksburg, Corinth, Memphis, Columbus, Kentucky

Letter 11   Date: October 22, 1863   Location: 15 miles west of Tuscumbia, Alabama

Officers mentioned: Colonel Torrence (killed), Captain Creighton
Units mentioned: 30th Iowa Infantry
Places mentioned:

Sam's Civil War

Letter 12   Date: December 2, 1863   Location: Chattanooga

    Officers mentioned:
    Units mentioned: 7th Ohio, 30th Iowa Infantry
    Places mentioned: Mission Ridge, Tennessee; White Oak Ridge, Georgia; Lookout Mountain, Tennessee; Huntsville, Alabama

Letter 13   Date: December 31, 1863   Location: Woodville, Alabama

    Officers mentioned: Lieutenant Bence
    Units mention: Company F
    Places mentioned: Bridgeport

Letter 14   Date: January 9, 1864   Location: Paint Rock River, Alabama

    Officers mentioned: Captain Creighton
    Units mentioned: 3rd Division
    Places mentioned: Huntsville

Letter 15   Date: January 28, 1864   Location: Camp Proclamation Paint Rock River, Alabama

    Officers mentioned:
    Units mentioned: Company C 30th Iowa Infantry
    Places mentioned: Nashville, Tennessee; Davenport

Letter 16   Date: February 4, 1864   Location: Paint Rock River, Alabama

Officers mentioned: Lieutenant Colonel Roberts
Units mentioned: 30th Iowa Infantry Volunteers, 14th Iowa
Places mentioned: Fort Donaldson; Columbus, Kentucky; Kossuth

Letter 17   Date: February 7, 1864   Location: Paint Rock River, Alabama

Officers mentioned: Lieutenant Colonel Roberts
Units mentioned: Ohio Regiments
Places mentioned: Young's Point, Louisiana; Tennessee River; Guntersville, Alabama; Kingston

Letter 18   Date: February 14, 1864   Location:

Officers mentioned:
Units mentioned:
Places mentioned:

Letter 19   Date: February 22, 1864   Location: Paint Rock Creek, Alabama

Officers mentioned: Captain Creighton, Colonel Roberts, General Osterhaus
Units mentioned: Company G, 13th Army Corps, First Iowa Battery, Company E
Places mentioned: Huntsville, Woodville, Chattanooga, Larkinsville, Scottsboro, Stevenson, Bridgeport

Sam's Civil War

Letter 20   Date: February 25, 1864   Location: Paint Rock River, Alabama

    Officers mention:
    Units mentioned:
    Places mentioned:

Letter 21   Date: March 21, 1864   Location: Woodville, Alabama

    Officers mentioned: General Osterhaus, Corporal Ganaway
    Units mentioned: 25th Iowa, Company E 1st Iowa, 14th Iowa, First Iowa Battery
    Places mentioned: Burlington, Iowa; Kossuth

Letter 22   Date: March 28, 1864   Location: Woodville, Alabama

    Officers mentioned:
    Units mentioned:
    Places mentioned:

Letter 23   Date: March 5, 1864   Location: Vicksburg
(David Heizer's letter to his parents -- Copied by Sam)

Letter 24   Date: May 1, 1864   Location: Woodville, Alabama

    Officers mentioned:
    Units mentioned:
    Places mentioned: Trianna, Alabama; Huntsville, Alabama; Woodville; Madison Station; Chattanooga, Stevenson

Letter 25   Date: May 20, 1864   Location: Kingston, Georgia

           Officers mentioned:
           Units mentioned:
           Places mentioned: Kingston, Resaca

Letter 26   Date: July 7, 1864   Location: near the Chattahoochee River

           Officers mentioned:
           Units mentioned:
           Places mentioned: Chattahoochee River

Letter 27   Date: August 5, 1864   Location: Near Atlanta

           Officers mentioned: Captain Samuel B. Heizer
           Units mentioned:
           Places mentioned: Kennesaw Mountain, Marietta

Letter 28   Date: August 17, 1864   Location: Near Atlanta, Georgia 1/2 mile to rear of

           Officers mentioned:
           Units mentioned: Company C, Company B
           Places mentioned: Vicksburg, Paint Rock

Letter 29   Date: August 25, 1864   Location: (Near Atlanta)
           This letter is about Sister Irene's death.

           Units mentioned: Second Brigade (1st Division)

Letter 30   Date: September 15,   Location: East Point,
            1864   Georgia

            Officers mentioned:
            Units mentioned:
            Places mentioned: Oxford, Mississippi

Letter 31   Date: October 18, 1864   Location: Chattanooga

            Officers mentioned: General Schofield, Colonel
            Stanley, Colonel Roberts
            Units mentioned:
            Places mentioned: Dalton; Resaca; Cleveland,
            Tennessee; Chattanooga

Letter 32   Date: October 24, 1864   Location: Chattanooga

            Officers mentioned: Hood, Sherman, Colonel
            Roberts, Captain Smith, Captain Watkins,
            General Steedman, Grant, Bragg, General Hooker,
            Osterhaus
            Units mentioned: 30th, 31st Iowa, 15th Army
            Corps, Osterhaus' Division (1st), Army of the
            Tennessee
            Places mentioned: Lookout Mountain,
            Chattanooga, Mission Ridge, Tennessee River,
            Summertown, Rock City, Lulu Falls

Letter 33   Date: Oct. 27, 1864   Location: Kingston,
                                     Georgia

            Officers mentioned: Colonel Roberts, Captain
            Croso, Corporal Cross

Units mentioned:
Places mentioned: Chattanooga; Dalton; Resaca; Atlanta; Kingston; Yellow Springs, Iowa

Letter 34   Date: December 18, 1864   Location: Near Savannah, Georgia

Officers mentioned: General Sherman, General Corse, Colonel Williamson, General Woods, General Hazen, Major General Kennards

Units mentioned: Company C, 2nd Brigade (Division 1), 4th Division, 4th Iowa, 2nd Division (15th Corps)

Places mentioned: Cave Springs, Rome, Vingings Station, Atlanta, Macon, Savannah Railroad, Savannah, Oconee River, Ogeechee River, Wright Bridge, Fort McAllister, Ossibow Sound

Letter 35   Date: Dec. 27, 1864   Location: Savanna, Georgia

Officers mentioned: Hood, General Sherman

Units mentioned: 15th Corps, 17th Corps, 14th Corps, 20th Corps

Places mentioned: Savannah, Chattanooga, Nashville

Letter 36   Date: January 22, 1865   Location: Near Beaufort, South Carolina

Officers mentioned:
Units mentioned:
Places mentioned:

Letter 37   Date: Jan. 28, 1865   Location: Near Beaufort, South Carolina

Officers mentioned:
Units mentioned:
Places mentioned:

Letter 38   Date: May 21, 1865   Location: Alexandria, Virginia

Officers mentioned: Sherman, General Washington
Units mentioned:
Places mentioned: Mount Vernon, Richmond, Alexandria, Capitol of the United States

Sam's Commanders

1862

The Regiment was organized at the Keokuk, Iowa September 20 to October 24. Sam was in Company C. Capt. Roberts was either the regiment or company commander.

October 25 through November

The Regiment was moved to St. Louis, Missouri and then to Helena, Arkansas.

Sam was in the 3rd Brigade, 11th Division, Right Wing, 13th Army Corps (Old).

Commanders:
- General S. R. Curtis/ General Frederick P. Steele
- Brigadier- General Alvan P. Hovey
- General Washburn - Cavalry
- General Wyman
- Col. Torrence - Regiment Field Officer

Early December 1862

Sam is in the 2nd Brigade, 4th Division, Department of the Tennessee

Commanders:
- Brigadier-General Fredrick Steele
- Colonel Torrence - Regiment Field Officer

Late December 1862

Sam is in the 3rd Brigade, 4th Division, Army of the Tennessee during W. T. Sherman's Yazoo Expedition, Vicksburg campaign.

Commanders:
- Major-General U. S. Grant - Army of the Tennessee
- Major-General William T. Sherman - 15th Army Corps
- Brigadier-General Fredrick P. Steele -Division
- Brigadier-General John M. Thayer - Brigade
- Captain Creighton - Regiment or Company

Sam's Civil War

1863

January through August

Sam was in the 3rd Brigade, 1st Division, 15th Army Corps, Department of the Tennessee Early January

Commanders:

    Major-General John A. McClernand - Army of the Mississippi

    Major-General W. T. Sherman - 2nd Corps

    General F. P. Steele - Division

    General J. M. Thayer - Brigade

General Grant was found to supercede General McClernand who was then assigned to the 13th Corps. The command then looked as follows:

    Major-General U. S. Grant - Commander Department of the Tennessee

    Major-General W. T. Sherman - 15th Army Corps

    General F. P. Steele/ General J. M. Thayer 1st Division

    General J. M. Thayer - Brigade

    Captain Roberts - Regiment - He replaced Col. Torrence.

September 1863 through August 1864

Sam was in the 2nd Brigade, 1st Division, 15th Army Corps, Army of the Tennessee.

Commanders:

    Major-General U. S. Grant - Army of the Tennessee

    Major-General W. T. Sherman - 15th Army Corps

    Brigadier-General Peter J. Osterhaus - 1st Division

    Colonel J. A. Williamson (4th Iowa) - Brigade

    Colonel Torrence - Regiment (Killed 10-21-63)

    Captain Creighton - Company

Commanders:

    Major-General W. T. Sherman - Army of the Tennessee (10-27-63)

    Major-General F. P. Blair - 15th Army Corps

    Major-General P. J. Osterhaus - 1st Division

Colonel J. A. Williamson (4th Iowa) Brigade
Lieutenant-Colonel Roberts - Regiment
Commanders:
    Major-General W. T. Sherman - Military Division of the Mississippi (3-18-64) This Army included the Departments of the Ohio, Cumberland, Tennessee, and Arkansas. These
    Departments were commanded respectively by Major-Generals Schofield, Thomas,
    McPherson, and Steele.
    Major-Generals James B. McPherson (killed 7-22-64)/ Oliver O. Howard - Army of the
    Tennessee (7-24-64)
    Major-General Charles R. Woods -1st Division
    Colonel J. A. Williamson - Brigade
    Commanders
    Lieutenant Colonel Roberts - Regiment

September 1864 Through July 1865

Sam was in the 3rd Brigade, 1st Division, 15th Corps, Army of the Tennessee (Right Wing).

In November 1864 The Army of the Mississippi was divided into two parts: the Right Wing which consisted of the 15th and 17th Army Corps commanded by Major-General O. O.

Howard and the Left Wing which consisted of the 14th and the 20th Corps and was commanded by Major-General Henry W. Slocum.

    Commanders:
    Major-General W. T. Sherman - Army of the Mississippi
    Major-General O. O. Howard - Army of the Tennessee - Right Wing (15th and 17th Corps)
    Major-Generals P. J. Osterhaus (10-64) / Brigadier-General promoted to Major-General
    John A. Logan (2-1-65) -15th Army Corps
    Brevet Major-General Charles R. Woods - 1st Division
    Colonel G. A. Stone - 3rd Brigade

The History of the 30th Iowa Regiment

The 30th Iowa was organized at Keokuk and mustard in September 20, 1862. They moved to St. Louis, Missouri, Oct. 25, 1862 and then to Helena, Arkansas. They were attached to the District of Eastern Arkansas, Department of Missouri, to December, 1862. The 30th Iowa was in the second Brigade, 1st Division, District of Eastern Arkansas, Department of Tennessee, December, 1862. They were then reorganized into the third Brigade, 11th Division, Right Wing 13th Army Corps (Old), Department of Tennessee. In Sherman's Yazoo Expedition, they were in the third Brigade, fourth Division to January, 1863. After another reorganization they were in the third Brigade, first Division, 15th Army Corps, Department of Tennessee, to September, 1863. The 30th Iowa was then placed in the second Brigade, 1st Division, 15th Corps, to December, 1863. They then became the first Brigade, first Division, 15th Corps to September, 1864.

The 30th Iowa Regiment began their service with an expedition from Helena, Arkansas, to Arkansas Post November 16-21, 1862. General Alvin P. Hovey led an expedition to Grenada, Mississippi, Nov. 27 to Dec. 5. On Dec. 1, some action took place at Mitchell's Cross Roads. They were with Sherman's Yazoo Expedition from December 22, 1862, to January 2, 1863. On Dec. 26-28, 1862 they were at the Chickasaw Bayou. They were at the Chickasaw Bluffs Dec. 29. The expedition to Arkansas Post, Arkansas was from Jan. 3-10, 1863. The assault on and capture of Fort Hindman, Arkansas Post, was from January 10-11. The 30th Iowa then moved to Young's Point, Louisiana, Jan. 17-23, and had duty there until April. The expedition to Greenville, Black Bayou and Deer Creek took place April 2-14. The demonstration on Haines and Snyder's Bluffs occurred

April 28-May 2. They then moved to join the Army in the rear of Vicksburg, Mississippi, by way of Richmond and Grand Gulf on May 2-14. They were involved in the assault on Jackson, Mississippi, May 14 and in the siege of Vicksburg May 18-July 4. They were also involved in the assaults on Vicksburg May 19 and 22. The 30th advanced on Jackson July 5-10 and laid siege to Jackson July 10-17. They pursued Joe Johnston's confederates to Brandon Station July 17-19. They then pulled back to the Big Black River and were there on duty until September 22. After they moved to Memphis, Tennessee they began the March to Chattanooga, Tennessee which took place from Sept. 22 to November 21. The regiment was involved in rebuilding the Memphis and Charleston Railroad in Alabama from October 20-29. They were at Cherokee Station on Oct. 21 and 29. On Oct. 26 they were at Cane Creek. They moved to Tuscumbia, Alabama Oct. 26-27. They were involved in the battles of Chattanooga on Nov. 23-27; Lookout Mountain Nov. 23-24; Mission Ridge Nov. 25; Ringgold Gap, Georgia; and Taylor's Ridge, Nov. 27. The regiment marched to the relief of Knoxville Nov. 28-Dec. 8. They were on garrison duty in Alabama until April, 1864. The Atlanta campaign began May 1 and lasted until Sept. 8. The demonstration on Resaca occurred May 8-13. The Battle of Snake Creek Gap happened May 10-12. The Battle of Resaca occurred May 14-15. The Army moved against Pumpkin Vine Creek and fought battles about Dallas, New Hope Church and Altoona Hills from May 25 to June 5. Actions around Marietta and against Kennesaw Mountain occurred June 10 to July 2. The attack on Bushy Mountain was from June 15-17. The assault on Kennesaw was on June 27. The battle of Nickajack Creek occurred Jul. 2-5. The action at the Chattahoochee River was from July 6-17. The Battle of Atlanta was fought July 22. The Siege of Atlanta lasted from July 22 to Aug. 25. The battle of Ezra Church and Hood's second sortie, happen July 28. A flank movement on Jonesboro was executed August 25-30. The Battle of Jonesboro lasted from August 31 to Sept. 1. The push to Lovejoy Station was from Sept. 2-6. The pursuit of Hood into Alabama occurred from October 1 to 26. The 30th Iowa marched to the sea with General Sherman from November 15 to December 10. They were at Griswoldsville Nov. 23. The Siege of Savannah occurred December 10-21. The campaign of the Carolinas lasted from January to April, 1865. This March involved the reconnaissance to the Salkehatchie River, South Carolina, Jan. 25; the Salkehatchie Swamps, South Carolina, Feb. 3-5; the crossing of the South Edisto River on Feb. 9; the crossing of the North Edisto River February 12-13. The Army entered Columbia, South Carolina February 15-17. They were at Lynche's Creek Feb. 25-26. The Battle of Bentonville, North Carolina happened March 20-21.

The army then occupied Goldsboro on March 24. The advance on Raleigh, North Carolina took place on April 9-13. Raleigh was occupied on April 14. The meeting at Bennett's House happened on April 26 where Confederate General Joe Johnston surrendered his army. The Army marched to Washington D.C. by way of Richmond, VA from April 29-May 20 and participated in the Grand Review on May 24. The soldiers were mustered out of the Army June 5, 1865.

During their service the Regiment lost eight officers and 65 enlisted men killed and mortally wounded and three officers and 241 enlisted men by disease. The total loss was 317 men.[60]

General William T. Sherman

Samuel B. Heizer's military career was served for the most part under the leadership of William Tecumseh Sherman. From December 1862 until the end of the war in April 1865 and through the Grand Review May 23 -24, 1865 in Washington D.C. General Sherman was his superior officer.

Sam came into the Army in September 1862. By that time Sherman had participated in the First Manassas battle or Bull Run as a brigade commander. He was a colonel. He was then made a Brigadier General serving in Kentucky in command of Union forces. In February 1862 he was given a division in the Army of the Tennessee which would become the second Division of the 15th Corps. General U. S. Grant was his commanding officer. During the Vicksburg campaign, late December 1862 to July 4, 1863, Sherman was a Major-General in command of the 15th Army Corps of the Army of the Tennessee.

On September 22, 1863 Grant ordered Sherman to march to Chattanooga, Tennessee to relieve a siege by Confederate forces in the wake of the union defeat at Chickamauga. After the Confederate siege was broken in late November the Confederates retreated into Georgia. While Sam wintered in northern Alabama, Sherman conducted a march from Vicksburg to Meridian in Mississippi. In March 1864, General Grant was promoted to lieutenant general, the highest rank in the Army, which was recently reinstated by Congress. Grant was then given command over all the armies while personally taking charge of the Army of the Potomac. Sherman was assigned the vacated command of Grant. This was the Military Division of the Mississippi and controlled the Departments of the Ohio, Cumberland, Tennessee, and Arkansas. In March Major-General James B. McPherson took command of the Army of the Tennessee.

General Sherman's campaign for Atlanta started on May 5, 1864 from Chattanooga. Battling Joe Johnston through northern Georgia Sherman arrived near Atlanta in early July. Atlanta then came under a state of siege, during which Joe Johnston turned over his command to General John Bell Hood. Four major battles were fought around Atlanta, the last of which at Jonesboro broke the siege of Atlanta on Sept. 1, 1864.

On September 21st Hood moved north hoping to disrupt Sherman's rail supply line. Sherman gave chase until Hood moved into Alabama and then on to Tennessee where he was defeated at Franklin and Nashville by General George Thomas.

General Sherman returned to Atlanta and by November 15 was on the move to Savannah. The troops experienced little opposition and reached Savannah December 9th and 10th. After a short siege the city was in Union hands on December 21st.

After a rest and refitting of about six weeks General Sherman began the march through the Carolinas starting about February 1, 1865. Marching through terrible conditions the Army reached Raleigh, North Carolina on April 13. Shortly afterward Sherman negotiated surrender terms with Joe Johnston.

At the end of the war Sherman was a Major-General commanding the Military Division of the Mississippi.

William T. Sherman prepared for military service by attending West Point academy. He graduated in 1840, sixth in his class. After his distinguished service in the Civil War, he became commander-in-chief of the U.S. Army. He is considered one of the most famous generals in history. His approach to warfare is considered the forerunner to modern military thinking.

William Tecumseh Sherman died of pneumonia in 1891 at the age of 71.[61]

Army of the Tennessee

The Army of the Tennessee was organized in October of 1862. The Army was made up of one corps, the XIII, which had 11 divisions and a cavalry unit. This structure was found to be unwieldy and was reorganized in December 1862. Four corps were created; the XIII, XV, XVI, and XVII; each was made up of two or three divisions with units of artillery and cavalry. The Army of the Tennessee was first commanded by General U.S. Grant who led the Army in the campaign against Vicksburg.

General William T. Sherman was given command of the Army of the Tennessee in October 1863, when Grant was moved to command the troops at Chattanooga, Tennessee. Sherman commanded the Army during the siege of Chattanooga, the Meridian campaign and other operations near Vicksburg. In March 1864, Sherman was given that command of the western armies which was preparing for a march on Atlanta. The Army of the Cumberland and the Army of the Ohio were joined with the Army of the Tennessee the latter being commanded by General James B. McPherson. The Army of the Mississippi, as it was called, moved from Chattanooga, Tennessee southward to Atlanta, Georgia. General McPherson was killed during the battle of Atlanta and General O. O. Howard assumed command during the rest of the war.

Southern resistance was light during the march from Atlanta to Savannah, Georgia and the campaign through the Carolinas. The Army had cut its own supply line at Atlanta and needed to live off the countryside. They created considerable havoc among the civilian population as a result. Public and private property was destroyed to help break the will for war of the Southern population. The rugged Western soldiers of the Army of the Tennessee were feared by many and earned a reputation second only to the much larger Army of the Potomac which fought only on the eastern front.

The war was essentially over for the soldiers of the Army of the Tennessee when their army, Army of the Tennessee, accepted to the surrender of General Joseph E. Johnston in late April 1865. In May they marched in the Grand Review in Washington D.C. Soon after the Army of the Tennessee was disbanded and ceased to exist. The Army never lost a major campaign and had what was probably the best combat record of any Union Army.[62]

UNION ARMY 15TH CORPS

(FROM FOX'S REGIMENTAL LOSSES CHAPTER VIII)

Chickasaw Bluffs; Arkansas Post; Deer Creek; Black Bayou; Snyder's Bluff; Jackson;
Assault on Vicksburg, May 19th; Assault on Vicksburg, May 22nd; Vicksburg Trenches;
Clinton; Jackson; Brandon; Cherokee; Tuscumbia; Lookout Mountain; Missionary Ridge;
Ringgold; Resaca; Dallas; Big Shanty; Kennesaw Mountain; Nickajack Creek; Battle of Atlanta;
Ezra Church; Jonesboro; Lovejoy's Station; Siege of Atlanta; Altoona Pass; Taylor's Ridge;
Griswoldville; Fort McAllister; River's Bridge; Congaree Creek; Columbia; Bentonville.

The Fifteenth Corps was one of the organization's resulting from the partition of the Thirteenth Corps, December 18, 1862. General William T. Sherman was assigned to its command. Part of the 15th Corps-- the divisions of Generals Steele and Morgan L. Smith, together with other troops -- were engaged under Sherman at Chickasaw Bluffs in the first attempt on Vicksburg. These two divisions lost in that action, 144 killed, 579 wounded, and 189 missing; total, 912. The entire loss of the Army at Chickasaw Bluffs was 1776. A few days later these two divisions accompanied McClernand's expedition to Arkansas Post, a successful affair which resulted in the capture of that place. General Sherman was present with those two divisions of his corps; General M. L. Smith having been severely wounded at Chickasaw Bluffs, his division was commanded at Arkansas Post by General David Stewart. The loss of the Fifteenth Corps in this affair was 86 killed, 501 wounded, and 11 missing; total 598. The loss of the entire Army was 1061.

During the spring of 1863 the Corps participated in the Bayou expeditions about Vicksburg, preceding the campaign in the rear of that city. On that campaign the Corps was composed of the three divisions of Steele, Blair, and Tuttle, numbered respectively as the First, Second, and Third Divisions; they were previously known as the Eleventh, Fifth, and Eighth, of the Army of the Tennessee. These three divisions contained 41 regiments of infantry, seven batteries of light artillery (36 guns), and five companies of cavalry, numbering in all, 15,975 present for duty, out of 19,238 present in the aggregate. Present and absent, it numbered 27,416 men.

Of the series of battles in the rear of Vicksburg, the battle of Jackson, May 14, was the only one in which the Fifteenth Corps took part. In that action Tuttle's Division was slightly engaged, losing six killed, 22 wounded, and four missing. The corps was engaged, next, in the investment of Vicksburg. In the assault of May 19th, it lost 134 killed, 571 wounded, and 8 missing; total, 713. In this assault the Fifteenth sustained the principal loss. The total of the casualties amounting to 942. In the general assault which occurred three days later-May 22nd-the Corps lost 150 killed, 666 wounded, and 42, missing total, 858. After the surrender of Vicksburg, the Army moved on to Jackson and invested that place; the corps losing there,-- July 10-16th,-- 10 killed, 32 wounded, and 38 missing. During the latter movement the First Division was commanded by General John M. Thayer.

After the evacuation of Jackson by the enemy, the Army returned to Vicksburg and its vicinity, the Fifteenth Corps encamping there until the latter part of September, when it moved to Memphis. The Third Division (Tuttle's) was left behind at Vicksburg, and it never rejoined the corps. Its place was taken by John E. Smith's Division (formerly Quinby's), Seventeenth Corps, which joined at Memphis and remained permanently attached, as the Third Division. William S. Smith's Division was detached from the Sixteenth Corps, becoming the Fourth Division. The four divisions having been concentrated at Memphis, moved thence to Chattanooga, where they participated in the battles of Lookout Mountain and Missionary Ridge, November 23-25, 1863. General Frank P. Blair was in command of the corps, General Sherman having been promoted, October 27, 1863, to the command of the three corps composing the Army of the Tennessee. The four divisions of the Fifteenth Corps were commanded at Missionary Ridge by Generals Osterhaus, Morgan L. Smith, John E. Smith, and Hugh Ewing. The losses of the corps in that battle, and the minor actions connected with it, aggregated 295 killed, 1402 wounded, and 292 missing; total 1989. After this battle the corps marched to the relief of Knoxville, arriving there December 6, 1863, two days after Longstreet's retreat. The corps then returned to Chattanooga, moving thence into Northern Alabama, where it went into winter quarters.

Under command of General Logan, it was actively engaged on the Atlantic campaign of 1864; its division commanders were Generals Osterhaus, Morgan L. Smith, John E. Smith, and Harrow. The Third Division (John E. Smith's) garrisoned points on Sherman's line of communication, and so was not present with the advancing columns. After the fall of Atlanta, Harrow's (4th) Division was consolidated with the others, and its place was taken by Corse's Division of the Sixteenth Corps. General Corse, with a provisional command from the Fifteenth Corps, made the famous defense of Allatoona Pass, an affair remarkable for the courageous, desperate fighting of commander, officers and men.

On the 12th of November, 1864, the Corps started with Sherman's Army on the march through Georgia to the sea. General Logan being absent, the Corps was under the command of General Osterhaus; the four divisions were commanded by Generals C. R. Woods, Hazen, John E. Smith, and Corse. They contained 60 regiments of infantry, and 4 batteries, the infantry numbering 15,894, present for duty; it was the largest corps in the Army that marched to the sea.

The Army of the Tennessee, under General Howard, formed the right wing of Sherman's Army as it marched through Georgia on its way to the sea, and was composed of the Fifteenth and Seventeenth Corps, only, that part of the Sixteenth Corps--2 divisions --which had served with the Army of the Tennessee on the Atlantic campaign having been consolidated with the two other corps. Although the three other corps in Sherman's Army marched uninterrupted to the sea, the Fifteenth had a brisk engagement at Griswoldville, in which Walcutt's Brigade, of Woods' Division repelled a determined attack; and again, upon reaching the sea, Hazen's Division was the one selected for the storming of Fort McAllister.

Savannah was evacuated December 21, 1864, after a short siege, and on the 1st of February, Sherman's Army started on its grand, victorious march through the Carolinas. General Logan having returned, he was again in command of his corps, which now numbered 15,755, infantry and artillery. It encountered some fighting in forcing disputed crossings at some of the larger rivers, and captured Colombia, SC., General C. R. Woods' Division occupying the city at the time it was burned. The corps was also in line at the battle of Bentonville, N. C., March 19, 1865; but General Slocum had won a substantial victory with his wing of the Army, and but little fighting, comparatively, devolved upon the Army of the Tennessee.

Johnston's Army having surrendered April 26th, the corps continued its northward march, and, arriving at Washington May 20th, participated in the Grand Review of May 24, 1865.

It proceeded, June 2nd, to Louisville, Ky., and in the latter part of the month the Second Division was ordered to Little Rock, Ark., where it served with the Army of Occupation. The organization was discontinued August 1, 1865.[63]

ARMY ORGANIZATION

To better understand the organizational structure of the Army during the Civil War, the following information is provided from Sherman's memoirs.[64]

A Company was made up of about 100 men. The company was a unit of discipline headed by a Captain. The Captain had the power to reward and punish. A Colonel or superior authority should appoint him.

A regiment was usually made up of a single battalion of ten companies and which usually had about 1000 men.

A brigade was made up of three regiments.

A division was made up of three brigades.

An Army Corps was made with three divisions. A corps was the unit for grand campaigns and battles and were commanded by a lieutenant general or often in the Civil War by a major general. When a corps is given a brigade of cavalry and six batteries of field artillery you have a *corps d' arme'e* of 30,000 men.

WESTERN THEATER ENGAGEMENTS (LIMITED)

1862

    January 19 -- Mill Springs, Kentucky

    February 6 -- Fort Henry

    February 13-15 -- Fort Donaldson

    March 8 -- Pea Ridge, Arkansas

    April 6-7 -- Shiloh or Pittsburgh Landing

    May 30 -- Corinth, Mississippi

    June 3 -- Fort Pillow (Memphis)

    July 13 -- Murfreesboro, Tennessee

    September 19 -- Iuka, Mississippi

    October 4 -- Corinth, Mississippi

    October 8-9 -- Perryville, Kentucky

    November 13 -- Holly Springs, Mississippi

    December 13 -- Tuscumbia, Alabama

    December 20 -- Holly Springs, Mississippi

    December 25 -- Sherman North of Vicksburg

    December 29 -- Chickasaw Bayou, Chickasaw Bluffs north of Vicksburg

1863

    December 31, 1862-Jan. 2 -- Battle of Stone's River or Murfreesboro

    January 11 -- Fort Hindman, Arkansas

February 1 -- Franklin, Tennessee

May 1 -- Port Gibson (Vicksburg)

May 16 -- Champion's Hill (Vicksburg)

May 17 -- Big Black River Bridge (Vicksburg)

July 4 -- Vicksburg surrender

July 8-9 -- Port Hudson, Louisiana surrender

September 19-20 -- Chickamauga

November 23-24 -- Chattanooga, Tenn.

November 25 -- Missionary Ridge, Tenn.

1864

March 2 -- Grant becomes General-in-Chief of U.S. Army

May 7 -- Sherman begins march to Atlanta

May 14-15 -- Battle of Resaca

May 25 -- New Hope Church

June 27 -- Kennesaw Mountain

July 14 -- Tupelo, Mississippi

July 20 -- Peachtree Creek

July 22 -- McPherson killed

August -- Atlanta Campaign

August 30 -- Jonesboro

September 1 -- Atlanta evacuated by South

October 10-11-12 -- Rome, Resaca, Georgia- Sherman chases Hood

October 20 -- (Thanksgiving declared a national holiday)

November 16 -- Sherman leaves Atlanta for "March to the Sea"

November 27 -- Siege of Petersburg

November 30 -- Franklin, Tennessee

December 13 -- Fall of Fort McAllister

December 20 -- Evacuation of Savannah by South

1865

January 10 -- Sherman orders move into South Carolina

February 1 -- March through Carolinas begins

February 15 -- Columbia, SC

March 16 -- Averysboro, North Carolina

March 19 -- Bentonville, NC

April 12 -- Lee surrenders

April 13 -- Sherman in Raleigh

April 14 -- Lincoln assassinated

April 26 -- Johnston surrenders

May 10 -- William Clark Quantrill killed in Taylorsville, Kentucky

May 13 -- Battle of Palmitto Ranch, Tex.

War Theater Comparisons (Limited)

WESTERN

1861

1862
- February 6 -- Fort Henry (Grant)
- February 13-16 -- Fort Donaldson (Grant)
- April 6-7 -- Shiloh or Pittsburg Landing (Grant)
- June 3 -- Fort Pillow (Grant)
- December 25 -- Begin Vicksburg Campaign (Grant)

1863
- Dec. 31, 1862-Jan. 2, 1863 -- Stone's River (Roscrans)
- July 4 -- Vicksburg surrenders (Grant)
- September 18-20 -- Chickamauga (Rosecrans)
- November 23 -- Orchard Knob at Chattanooga (Grant)
- November 24 -- Lookout Mountain (Grant)
- November 25 -- Missionary Ridge (Grant)
- November 26 -- Ringgold, Ga. (Grant)

EASTERN

1861
- April 14 -- Fort Sumpter
- July 21 -- Manassas - 1st Bull Run

1862
- May 31 -- Fair Oaks
- June 26-July 1 -- Day's Battle-Richmond, Va.
- August 28-30 -- 2nd Manassas
- September 17 -- Antietam (McClellan)
- Dec. 13 -- Fredricksburg (Burnside)

1863
- May 2-3 -- Chancellorsville (Hooker)
- May 4-5 -- Salem Church
- July 4 -- Gettysburg taken (Meade)

1864

May 14-15 -- Resacca (Sherman)
May 25 -- New Hope Church (Sherman)
June 22 -- Kolb's Farm (Sherman)
June 27 -- Kennesaw Mountain (Sherman)
July 20 -- Peachtree Creek (Sherman)
July 22 -- Battle of Atlanta (Sherman)
July 28 -- Ezera Church (Sherman)
September 1 -- Jonesboro (Sherman)

1865

February 15-20 -- Columbia, SC (Sherman)
March 16 -- Averysboro NC (Sherman)
March 19 -- Bentonville NC (Sherman)
April 26 -- Johnston surrenders at Bennett's House

1864

May 5-7 The Wilderness (Grant)
May 8-19 -- Spotsylvania (Grant)
June 3-13 -- Cold Harbor (Grant)
June 15-18 -- Petersburg (Grant)

1865

April 19 -- Lee Surrenders at (Sherman) Appomattox Court House (Grant)

BIBLIOGRAPHY

Carter III, Samuel. *The Siege of Atlanta*. New York: St. Martins Press, 1973.

Davis, Burk. *Sherman's March*. New York: Random House, 1980.

Korn, Jerry. *War on the Mississippi*. Alexandria, Virginia: Time Life Books, 1985.

Sherman, William T. *Memoirs of General William T. Sherman. (Vols. I & II)*. New York: Appleton, 1875. Introduction by William S. McFeely. United States of America: Da Capro Press, 1984.

http://www.civilwararchive.com/unionia.htm

http://iagenweb.org/civilwar/regiment/index.htm

http://www.sherpaguides.com/georgia/civil_war/sidebars/sherman.html

http://www.civilwarhome.com/15thcorps.htm

ENDNOTES

1. http://www.iowa-counties.com/civilwar/30th_inf/30th-inf-regimental_histort.htm (3/8/2002)
2. William T. Sherman, *Memoirs of General William T. Sherman. (Vols. 1 & 2)* (New York: Appleton, 1875), Vol. 1, 289-293.
3. Ibid. Vol. 1, 305.
4. Ibid., 319.
5. Ibid., 320-331.
6. Ibid., 332.
7. William T. Sherman. Memoirs of General William T. Sherman (New York: Appleton, 1875), Vol.1, 373.
8. http://iagenweb.org/civilwar/regiment/index.htm
9. William T. Sherman. Memoirs of General William T. Sherman. (New York: Appleton, 1975), Vol. 2, 5.
10. Ibid., 33-34
11. Ibid., 37, 43-44.
12. Ibid., 51,53.
13. Ibid., 60, 62, 65-67.
14. Ibid., 70-72.
15. William T. Sherman. *Memoirs of General William T. Sherman.* (New York: Appleton , 1875) Vol. 2, 75-77.
16. Ibid., Vol. 2, 79-81.
17. Ibid., Vol. 2, 82.
18. Ibid., Vol. 2, 85.
19. Ibid., Vol. 2, 89-91.
20. Ibid., Vol. 2, 99.
21. Ibid., Vol. 2, 102.
22. Ibid., Vol. 2, 104-105, 107-108.
23. Ibid., Vol. 2, 130.
24. Ibid., Vol. 2, 145.
25. Ibid., Vol. 2, 147.
26. Ibid., Vol. 2, 154-156, 159.
27. Ibid., Vol. 2, 158-159, 161.
28. Ibid., Vol. 2, 166.

29 William T. Sherman. *Memoirs of General William T. Sherman*. (New York: Appleton, 1875), Vol. 2, 171-175.
30 Ibid., Vol. 2, 178-179.
31 Ibid., Vol. 2, 187-188.
32 Ibid., Vol. 2, 190-191.
33 Ibid., Vol. 2, 193.
34 Ibid., Vol. 2, 194-196.
35 Ibid., Vol. 2, 198, 203-204, 210, 216-217, 231.
36 Ibid., Vol. 2, 227.
37 William T. Sherman. *Memoirs of General William T. Sherman*. (New York: Appleton, 1875), Vol. 2, 240-241.
38 Ibid., Vol. 2, 253.
39 Ibid., Vol. 2, 268.
40 Ibid., Vol. 2, 272-274.
41 Ibid., Vol. 2, 275-277.
42 Ibid., Vol. 2, 279.
43 Ibid., Vol. 2, 280.
44 Ibid., Vol. 2, 288, 290, 292-294.
45 Ibid., Vol. 2, 295.
46 Ibid., Vol. 2, 297.
47 Ibid., Vol. 2, 300-302.
48 Ibid., Vol. 2, 303-304.
49 Ibid., Vol. 2, 306-307.
50 Ibid., Vol. 2, 328, 333-335.
51 Ibid., Vol.2, 341-344.
52 Ibid., Vol. 2, 344.
53 Ibid., Vol. 2, 345.
54 Ibid., Vol. 2, 346-347, 348-354.
55 Ibid., Vol. 2, 358, 362.
56 William T. Sherman. *Memoirs of General William T. Sherman*. (New York: Appleton , 1875), 374-376.
57 Ibid., Vol. 2, 376.
58 Ibid., Vol. 2, 377-378.
59 Ibid., Vol. 2, 379-380.
60 http://www.civilwararchive.com/unionia.htm
61 http://www.sherpaguides.com/georgia/civil_war/sidebars/sherman.html

[62] William T. Sherman. *Memoirs of General William T. Sherman* (New York: Appleton, 1875).

[63] http://www.civilwarhome.com/15thcorps.htm

[64] William T. Sherman. *Memoirs of General William T. Sherman* (New York: Appleton, 1875), Vol. 2, 383-385.